CRYSTAL AND GEMSTONE
Divination

Your Guide to Reading the Energies of the Mineral Realm for Life Guidance, Health and Well-Being

GAIL BUTLER

Gem Guides Book Company

Copyright © 2008
Gem Guides Book Company

All rights reserved. No part of this book may be reproduced or transmitted in any form by any electronic or mechanical means, photocopying or recording, including information and retrieval systems, without permission in writing from the publisher, except for inclusions of brief quotations in a review.

Library of Congress Control No.: 2008929354
ISBN 978-1-889786-42-1

Book Layout and Design: Dianne Nelson, Shadow Canyon Graphics
Cover Design: Scott Roberts

Published in the United States of America
Printed in China

PUBLISHERS NOTE
Neither the publisher nor the author make any warranties as to the accuracy or benefits of any applications described herein in any individual case. In cases of serious physical or mental health concerns you should always consult your physician, alternative practitioner or psychologist.

Published by
Gem Guides Book Company
315 Cloverleaf Drive, Suite F
Baldwin Park, CA 91706
www.gemguidesbooks.com

Contents

INTRODUCTION vii

CHAPTER 1: The Nature of Mineral Consciousness........................... 1
 Minerals and the Evolution of the Earth 5
 Minerals and the Evolution of Humankind 6
 The Nature and Actions of Minerals 9
 The Evolution of Crystals and Gemstones 11

CHAPTER 2: The Hidden Messages Within Crystals and Gemstones............ 17
 Origins and Messages of Crystals and Gemstones 18

CHAPTER 3: What Is Crystal and Gemstone Divination?...................... 63
 The Basics of Reading the Stones 66
 How the Gemstone Selection Process Works 68
 Keeping Records 71
 Ethics of Giving a Crystal and Gemstone Reading 72

CHAPTER 4: The Self-Reading and Gemstone Interpretation 77
 Record Keeping for Learning and Self-Transformation 78
 Interpretation of Gemstone Messages 79
 The Self-Reading and Personal Transformation 93

CHAPTER 5: Reading Crystals and Gemstones for Others..................... 97
 Reading the Pad 99
 Readings from My Client Files 102

CHAPTER 6: Gemstone Forecasting and Other Divination Systems 125

CHAPTER 7: Acquiring, Energizing, and Caring for Crystals and Gemstones 143
New Age Shops   145
Rock Shops   145
Gem and Mineral Shows   145
On-Line   147
Other Sources   147
Care and Cleansing of Crystals and Gemstones   147
Energizing of Crystals and Gemstones   154
Storing Your Crystals and Gemstones   157

CHAPTER 8: Other Uses for Your Crystals and Gemstones 159
Meditation and Visualization with Your Divination Stones   159
Crystal and Gemstone Dreamwork   165
Chakra Balancing   168
Amulets and Talismans   172
Raising and Elevating Energy   173

CHAPTER 9: Substitution and Gemstone Programming..................... 175
The Silica Factor   176
Programming Crystals and Gemstones   180
Adding Potential Message Categories   181
The Power of Attraction   182
Listening to Crystals and Gemstones   184

CHAPTER 10: Water Magnetism, Dowsing, and Gemstone Elixirs 187
Healing and Crystals and Gemstones   187
Crystals, Gemstones and Physical Healing   188
Water Magnetism and Gemstone Healing   190
Water Magnetism and Gemstone Elixirs   191
Healing Properties of Gemstone Elixirs   194
Dowsing and Auric Enhancement   198

GLOSSARY	203
BIBLIOGRAPHY	204
SOURCES	206
INDEX	208
ABOUT THE AUTHOR	214

Introduction

• • • • • • • • • • • • •

While much has been written about the metaphysical and healing attributes of gemstones and crystals, surprisingly very little information is available about using crystals and gemstones for divination. Yet, "casting the stones" to divine the future is an age-old craft still practiced in many parts of the world today.

Divination with crystals and stones is an all but forgotten art in most industrialized cultures. However, to our forebears they were of great importance as a means of divining the future. Casting the stones was as important as their other uses for magic, healing, spiritual protection, and weapon making. It is but a small step from using stones for healing, meditation, or chakra balancing to employing them in forecasting the nature and type of events looming upon the horizon of the present moment.

Crystal and gemstone divination is similar in many respects to other popular types of foretelling, such as tarot cards and rune stones. Yet, for most people, crystal and gemstone divination is easier to learn because of the natural resonance between humans and the mineral kingdom. Their beauty, color, and the way they feel in hand or worn upon the body entrances and delights. This affinity between the mineral realm and humankind is a two-way path. We only need reawaken to the hidden language of gemstones and crystals. Our ancestors communicated with the mineral realm and so can we.

An easily learned method of communication between mineral and human is crystal and gemstone divination. Using the techniques revealed in this book you will be able to use crystals and gemstones to predict the future, receive mineral wisdom, and detect and avert potential health problems. By knowing ahead of time that frequencies of impending health ailments are germinating in the aura, steps may be taken to avert them so they don't anchor in the physical body. Just having a clue that a health problem is pending allows one to take preventative steps using methods suggested by the crystals and gemstones themselves!

Additionally, selected stones from a divination set may be carried or worn in a small pouch to assist in manifestation, invigorating the aura, and increasing personal magnetism, as needed. Also, stones may be selected that will draw prosperity, attract love, deflect negative energy, or enhance meditation and dream recall. Crystals and gemstones may be used to make healing elixirs to benefit the body.

Methods for reading crystals and gemstones are easy to learn. Through the use of photographs, illustrations, and examples of actual divinations readers will effortlessly learn and understand the simple and effective crystal and gemstone foretelling techniques revealed in this book.

Crystals and gemstones have a long and noble history of use as talismans and amulets worn or carried for protection or to attract any number of desirable energies to the wearer. Ancient cultures worldwide have used various crystals and gemstones in healing rituals and ceremonies and for casting in order to predict if a hunt would be successful or fraught with danger.

Most cultures have had a system wherein the energies of crystals and stones were used as aids on a variety of levels. For most industrialized cultures these techniques have been lost or relegated to the realms of superstition. There remain a few cultures that still practice divination with gemstones and crystals, a practice that is as old as humankind because it works!

My own Cherokee ancestors dropped clear quartz crystals into cisterns and pools to keep water pure, fresh tasting, and disease-free. Spiritual leaders of the various villages of the Cherokee Nation utilized special quartz crystals to augur events for the upcoming year and to locate herds of wild game. These crystals "told" which direction and how far to travel to find the herds necessary to the villagers' survival. And, it was common for individuals to wear or carry a special crystal or gemstone that "spoke" in a sacred way to that individual.

Similarly, by using a beautiful selection of natural and tumble-polished quartz crystals and semi-precious gemstones we allow that same mineral wisdom—a wisdom that will help guide us to a more healthful, prosperous, and positive future—to speak to us.

I invite you to sojourn with me into the world of crystals and gemstones, to learn their language, to understand what they have long been trying to communicate, and to receive and understand their ageless wisdom. I will share what I have learned about how various Earth elements form into minerals and rocks that have specific tasks in helping the Earth and all that is upon it – including humans – to evolve!

On this journey you will learn how to assemble your own divination set and ask for and receive clear answers to your questions about life and love, about health, and about your future.

If you already use another divination system you will discover how to seamlessly harmonize crystal and gemstone forecasting with your present system. You will also learn important but simple techniques for accessing both mineral wisdom and healing by using particular crystals and gemstones from your divination set.

And, you will discover which gemstones best allow access to specific types of information and, in the event that certain stones prove unattainable in your area, how to substitute for others with similar properties or to "program" stones to provide what is needed.

Each and every journey begins with a first step. Let us begin this very moment the wonderful, mystical journey into the magical and enigmatic realms of the mineral kingdom!

Dedication

*This book is dedicated to the Mineral Realm.
Thank you for teaching of wondrous things;
for beauty and color added to life;
for shelter, nourishment, healing;
for messages of the future;
for wisdom and advice;
and for decades of adventure and
exploration of Earth's mountains,
shores, and deserts where
mineral-beings are found
in abundance in
their natural places.*

CHAPTER 1

The Nature of Mineral Consciousness

MINERALS ARE CONSCIOUS AFTER A MANNER. They have life of a sort, although mineral life cannot be described by any of the terms we use to define human, animal, or plant life.

Mineral life is of a nature we are unfamiliar with because it is inorganic and inanimate. Yet humans and minerals can communicate. Accepting the premise that we live in an "aware" universe will make the concept of mineral consciousness and inter-realm communication more fathomable as we explore the mineral-human connection.

There exists an all but forgotten channel of communication between the mineral realm and humanity. This channel was well known by our ancestors who utilized stones of all types in their daily lives for tools, weapons, jewelry, building materials, shamanic work and divination.

Despite our reliance on technology, we modern-day humans are just as capable of tuning in to the mineral realm as our ancient ancestors. Science and technology, wonderful as they make day-to-day life, have, in

Minerals are conscious but it is a form of consciousness unfamiliar to us.

1

many cases, anesthetized us to life's mysteries. We have forgotten, and in most cases rejected outright, many of our ancient birthrights—communication with the mineral realm is one such.

To our detriment we have accepted the premise that communication with other realms is impossible, or irrational. This belief has closed the portal that once connected us to the whole of creation. Science brings wonderful benefits but can also blind us to other, subtler ways of knowing.

By re-awakening to the concept that communication with other realms is possible we take the first step in making it so. Then, through attention and conscious receptivity, we begin to rebuild a connection that allows inter-realm dialog.

Crystals and gemstones have messages they want to share with us. These messages are about hope, wisdom, healing and the future, and hold great benefit for humankind collectively and individually. There is nothing difficult about tuning into the mineral realms. The remarkable thing is that it is so simple. It is as if minerals have been waiting for us to open up and receive their messages!

The first step to attunement is to merely observe and handle crystals and gemstones with appreciation and respect. This was how it all started for me over thirty years ago. My work as a mineral collector, gem hunter and gold prospector put me into profound physical contact with the mineral realm. I hunted for interesting minerals and crystals, and prospected for gold, spending lots of time outdoors in mountains and deserts.

My interest in collecting and appreciation for the beauty and variety of minerals and gemstones encouraged me to research and locate sites where they are found. Taking my finds home I cleaned, displayed, or cut and polished them into beautiful pieces of jewelry and art.

Author prospecting for gold

THE NATURE OF MINERAL CONSCIOUSNESS 3

Meanwhile, something was happening as I collected and worked with crystals and gemstones. It was little things at first, subtle things—such as a mysterious infusion of energy when I was tired or an intuitive message suddenly popping into my head that came true.

Yet, most of these unusual events passed through my awareness labeled as "coincidences." I simply had no context by which to understand them. Furthermore, I had yet to attribute these remarkable effects with a particular cause. Gradually I became more mindful of effects as they began to occur with greater frequency. Things became more obvious when working for long periods of time with certain types of stones, mostly agate and jasper—members of the silicate family—stones that are rich in silica, the mineral-component of quartz. And then there were the cats...

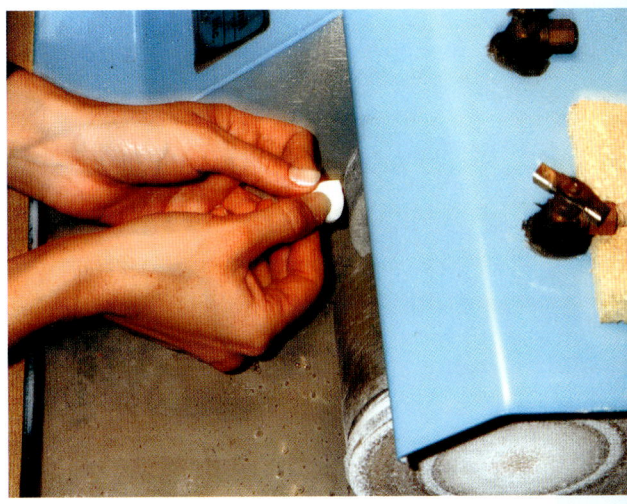

Polishing gemstones for jewelry put me into profound contact with gemstone energies.

I've always shared my life with one or more cats, and for a busy person who

Orangina loved the energy of the crystals on the workbench in my lapidary shop.

travels and works a lot, cats proved to be low-maintenance, affectionate pets. I began noticing that the cats were attracted to a flat basket of crystals sitting atop the workbench in my lapidary shop. Sometimes a questing paw would push a particular crystal about for minutes at a time. Most often a cat would curl up against the basket, sometimes sleeping with its head draped over the crystals inside.

My journey of communication with crystals and gemstones was born out of a purely material interest in the mineral kingdom. A great deal of skepticism had to be suspended in order to delve into the mineral realm in a radical new way. My training in the geological sciences had not prepared me for metaphysical contacts with minerals. Still, I didn't fight what I was discovering—or being discovered by—although trying to find some way of pinning a rational explanation on it was proving problematic. Finally I simply had to abandon the notion that something unsanctioned by science could not have validity.

Unable to pursue my findings scientifically, I tried a metaphysical approach and found that by simply opening my mind to possibility that portals to the mineral realm began to open. Communication arose first by physical contact. I found that holding a stone and just gently focusing my mind upon it facilitated a better connection. Then I tried meditating with the stones and this opened a clearer link. Messages soon began to come through dreams if I placed a stone beneath my pillow for several nights and focused attention on it until falling asleep. After a time my channel to the mineral realm became clearer and more immediate, particularly with stones with which I had already established a physical connection. It is when I began to "hear" the messages of crystals and gemstones during normal waking consciousness—not just in meditations or dreams—that I realized something truly extraordinary was occurring!

> My own strong attraction to quartz crystals made these a special favorite of mine and I was always on the lookout for nice specimens. I knew that ancestors from the Cherokee side of my family used quartz crystals in particular ways. I imagined that my passion for them was due in part to their beauty and possibly even some residual race-memory embedded in my DNA.

Minerals and the Evolution of Earth

Fundamental elements combine to create minerals that are the components of rocks and stones. This in itself is not remarkable. Every geologist and anyone who's taken a class in earth sciences know this. What is remarkable is that individual minerals and their compounds are aware and have specific functions to perform relative to the evolution of the Earth and everything on it, including humans.

Minerals actively participate in the Earth's evolution, but on a geologic time scale whose vastness is beyond human perception. The human life span is simply not long enough to observe evolution on this epochal time line. Yet, the science of geology proves that the Earth is modified over time by changes and alterations to its topography.

When vast sheets of rock are uplifted by geologic stress, mountains are formed. Time and erosion will eventually wear these mountains away. Coastal areas change configuration as land erodes or is built up through tectonic or volcanic activity. Rivers change course and carve out gorges transporting minerals to new locations. Continents gradually move and drift over the face of the planet. New islands form when oceanic volcanoes disgorge mineral-rich magma.

Minerals are an important part of this dynamic. Combinations of elements—mineral compounds that include oxygen and carbon dioxide—form the rocks that are the geography, or body, of our planet. Earth-processes break down rocks and recombine their elements and minerals. Out of rocks are born crystals and gemstones with their more complex and refined vibratory frequencies. Crystals and gemstones influence the planet and life on Earth in subtle ways and with more rarified intent, focus, and purpose than singular mineral components. Through the agency of minerals, mineral combinations, and dynamic Earth processes our planet evolved from a molten ball of seething lava into a miraculous planet that could support an astonishing diversity of life.

> When we incorporate minerals, crystals and gemstones into our lives we are subject to their subliminal energies in the form of vibrations. Each Earthly element vibrates to a specific frequency. When minerals combine, their individual frequencies create various effects and conditions upon the Earth.

We use minerals daily. Our homes are built of products containing them. We ingest minerals in food and water. Minerals are constituents within our bodies. There is no aspect of life wherein minerals do not have some role to play. We are literally made up of the substance of the Earth!

In addition to each mineral's physical role upon the Earth and within our bodies each has its particular mission to fulfill on a metaphysical or vibrational level, based upon its component elements. Each mineral has a memory and a mission carried as a unique vibration, or oscillation, within its energy signature.

In the case of minerals bound with the atoms of gases, chemicals, or other minerals, their roles—or properties—may be binary, tertiary, or greater. Science and industry accepts this although the deeper implications remain, as yet, undiscovered.

In industry elements are isolated or "refined" out of minerals and ores. The resulting pure products are used to make useful alloys for various purposes. Some minerals temper, strengthen, create malleability, and in other ways have properties that make them useful in technology. It is these and other qualities of minerals that also affect the course of evolution on our planet.

Within the disciplines of science and industry there is cerebral knowledge of the molecular differences that give minerals certain unique properties. However, their subtle vibrational characteristics of memory and purpose remain undiscovered and unacknowledged by today's technologies. Nor are minerals usually used in their holistic form by science or industry. Holistically, mineral elements and their compounds affect the evolution of the Earth, the animal and plant kingdoms, and the human body in their unpurified and unprocessed forms.

Minerals and the Evolution of Humankind

Minerals in the configurations of crystals and gemstones have a greater impact upon the evolution of the group consciousness of humankind than do single mineral elements and simple compounds which tend, instead, to effect physical evolution and forms.

Wearing gemstones has only a very subliminal effect upon individual consciousness if done purely for adornment. Wearing or carrying, meditating with, or using crystals with intention allows us greater exposure to their sublime evolutionary impulses. It is on the level of intention that we may best communicate with this realm. For the

THE NATURE OF MINERAL CONSCIOUSNESS

purposes of healing, meditation, and divination, natural minerals, crystals, and gemstones are used. They may also be polished and shaped to achieve their highest beauty and attractiveness to humankind.

Polishing and shaping does not affect their inherent vibrations. It is because of their vibrations that crystals and gemstones may heal us, communicate with us, and help us evolve if we are open to these possibilities. Nothing is ever forced upon us. We have a choice to open to or to block the energies of crystals and gemstones. If we do not intentionally engage with the vibrations of the mineral kingdom we receive only mediocre effects.

Many of us unwittingly block beneficial gemstone energies through an unawareness that it is necessary to ask or hold the intention for interaction. Asking opens the door to the mineral realm and increases the benefits received. In this way, we can enhance our own personal evolution of consciousness. We intensify and more directly focus mineral energy when we choose to wear or use crystals, gemstones, and jewels with intention and respect.

It is in the form of crystals and gemstones that the mineral realm expresses its highest level of evolution for both the planet and human beings.

While individual and simple compounds of minerals surround us environmentally and are components of our physical bodies and the soil around us, crystals and gemstones affect us on subtler metaphysical levels through our auras and energy

The mineral realm expresses its highest level of evolution through crystals and gemstones

centers, or chakras. By stimulating the charkas, crystals and gemstones can initiate the energy of healing.

Crystals and gemstones heighten and direct energy stimulating mental, emotional and psychic results. Through their ability to refine and elevate mineral energy, crystals and gemstones are assisting our species in its evolution, particularly if we are willing, receptive participants. There was a lot more going on during the Stone Age than scientists are likely or willing to understand! Our ancient ancestors did understand, however, and so do members of some cultures today.

We marvel at how Stone Age people were able to shape and erect massive stone structures. We do not understand how this was accomplished when even our modern machinery would be sorely taxed to move and hoist the stones moved by our "primitive" ancestors. While I cannot tell you how ancient people accomplished their amazing feats, I can tell you that it was with cooperation from the mineral realm. The mineral realm told the ancients how to achieve what to us appear to be seemingly impossible tasks!

The Greek culture was shaped by marble. Through the sophisticated vibratory influences of vast marble deposits the Greeks reached great pinnacles of refinement in both art and architecture.

> Not only did the mineral realm aid the ancients but it also aided in their evolution depending upon the types of rocks and minerals that predominated in areas out of which particular cultures sprang. Think of the diversity of architecture styles of several of the prominent historical cultures we still admire today.

The Romans did not have extensive deposits of marble, but out of the volcanic ash that predominated around Rome they created a sturdy type of concrete that set under water and was used to pave roads for commerce and transport of war machines. Cement enabled the Romans to build cisterns and aqueducts that brought water from afar for plumbing, drinking, and water fountains. They built impressive cities, parts of which still stand today, out of bricks held together by their incredibly durable concrete mortar saving what little marble they did have for facades and temples. Out of the influence and use of the minerals inherent to their environment arose a strong, militaristic nation of empire builders that conquered much of the known world. Think of the vast expanses of cement with which we pave our world today and wonder how its overuse might be influencing our own evolution. While cement is a wonderful, useful building medium, too much of it might have implications for the type of future we are building for ourselves.

Sandstone was the building and evolutionary medium of the Egyptians whose mathematical skills enabled them to erect amazingly accurate and geometrically precise structures. Of the Seven Wonders of the World, the Great Pyramid is the only one that still remains for us to gaze at and wonder upon. Sandstone aided the Egyptians not only in attempting to create buildings that would last for eternity, but in influencing their desire to "eternalize" their bodies through embalming and mummifying so that they, too, might have eternal "life." We think of these cultures as creating unique art forms and grand styles of architecture. What really happened here is that the architecture of these and other cultures is instead an expression of the properties of the rocks and minerals indigenous to the areas from which civilizations arose.

Today, we rarely build and create culture from the rocks beneath our feet. Globally, most modern buildings are built of steel and concrete which are products for import and export. We are, architecturally speaking, becoming a "mono-architectural" culture. This may have interesting connotations for humankind. We might want to ask ourselves what this could mean for our evolution. Perhaps one result is that our richly diverse cultures might meld into a single, global society with a few minor regional differences.

The Nature and Actions of Minerals

In addition to helping humankind's evolution there are messages the mineral realm is willing to share with us collectively and as individuals. First however, we need to understand more about the nature of minerals and the action of each.

Following is a brief list of the basic elements that make up minerals, rocks, gemstones and crystals. In parentheses behind each element is its chemical symbol. Some of these substances don't occur in nature in their pure form but exist as compounds of more than one chemical element. As an example, aluminum must be isolated out of rocks (ores) containing it, such as bauxite, which is itself a combination of elements, with silica, and clay. Fluorine is another element that only occurs in nature in a compounded form.

10 CRYSTAL AND GEMSTONE DIVINATION

A "force" or "energy" manifesting at various frequencies is what gives each mineral its unique properties. Furthermore, each element's vibration may be modified depending upon whether it has a predominantly negative or positive charge and the polarity of the surrounding atoms and molecules. The following will give you an idea of the types of polarity-based functions inherent in individual elements within minerals:

Element	Energy
Aluminum (Al)	Conductive/Reflective
Beryllium (Be)	Compressive/Resistive
Calcium (Ca)	Amplification/Absorption
Chlorine (Cl)	Purgation/Attraction
Chromium (Cr)	Resistance/Tempering
Copper (Cu)	Conductivity/Elasticity
Fluorine (F)	Flowing/Reactive
Gold (Au)	Non-reactive/Malleable
Iron (Fe)	Grounding/Morphological
Lithium (Li)	Subduing/Transferring
Magnesium (Mg)	Insulate/Conflagrant
Manganese (Mn)	Re-directive/Resistive/Reductive
Potassium (K)	Reaction/Fusion
Silver (Ag)	Reflective/Reactive
Sulfur (S)	Adhesion/Vulcanization
Silica (Si)	Transmission/Storage
Sodium (Na)	Reactive/Absorptive
Titanium (Ti)	Movement/Non-corrosive/Refractive
Zinc (Zn)	Stabilizing/Receptive

These are only a few of the many Earth elements but they are some of the common components that make rocks, stones, crystals and gemstones. When we understand how the singular energies of individual and compound elements manifest, we begin to comprehend the much more complex vibrational properties embodied in crystals and gemstones.

Then there are the processes—the dynamic forces—to which minerals were and are subjected to that form them into the rocks that compose the "bones" of our planet. Out of mineral-rich rock, crystals and gemstones evolve and grow. Each stone with its unique combination of minerals has been created as the result of dynamic Earth-processes, processes that confer both experience, potential, and mineral memory.

The Evolution of Crystals and Gemstones

Let's journey back in time and witness how dynamic Earth-processes give rise to crystals and gemstones. The actions of wind—and water as liquid, ice, or frost—are important processes to which rocks are subjected.

Across vast eras of time both wind and water scoured and gradually wore away rocks into small particles carrying these over distances. Particles in the form of sediment, dust, mud, and sand slowly accumulated in new locations.

In some places leaves, insects, shells, and bones of long-extinct animals were caught between continually accumulating

Dynamic Earth-processes such as water break apart solid rock, eventually reducing it to rubble, sand and dust.

layers of dust and sand. These organic bits decayed leaving voids. Into the voids various minerals percolated, such as silica (eroding out of silica-rich magmas and rocks) preserving the configurations of once living creatures but not their original substance.

Time passed.

As layers of rock-sediment built upon existing layers, the accumulated weight and pressure created heat. Under pressure and heat the particles became elastic and malleable lightly cementing together. Percolation from rainwater into minute cracks and fissures introduced mineral-rich precipitate that also acted to bond particles more firmly. Layering and bonding of diverse materials resulted in a type of rock called "sedimentary."

Sedimentary rock may be a few feet or many hundreds of feet thick and is the type of rock in which most fossils are found. Earthquakes, freezing and thawing, and more weathering by wind and rain created and widened fissures in sedimentary rock. Rains falling throughout the ages percolated down into widening cracks and fissures carrying mineral matter and introducing new combinations of elements to the mix. These processes, though spoken of in the past tense, are continual and ongoing and will in time alter and transform the Earth anew.

Eventually within sedimentary rocks minute crystals began to form, growing unseen in darkness and mystery. Crystals and fossils slumbered within the interstices of sedimentary rock deposits throughout ages beyond comprehension.

The sedimentary mineral realm will help you "settle" issues, resolve conflicts through compromise, and calm and soothe "unsettled" emotions. They will help you withstand the "pressure" of deadlines and responsibilities and help you see beyond the immediate moment.

Crystals and gemstones born out of sedimentary rock have wisdom inherent to the particular minerals of which they are composed and the manner by which they were formed—settling, weight and pressure.

In many places on Earth volcanoes erupted, spewing mineral-rich magma from molten places deep beneath the ground. Some of this material—silica—solidified rapidly creating a natural glass called, "obsidian." Magma containing denser minerals extruded upon the surface of the Earth and began to cool and harden into a rock called "basalt." Minerals born of Earth's fiery processes, such as volcanism, are called "igneous" rocks.

THE NATURE OF MINERAL CONSCIOUSNESS 13

Time beyond human comprehension passed.

Earthquakes, and freezing and thawing of moisture created cracks and fissures in mineral-rich basalts. These began to wear down under the scouring assault of wind and time. Minerals eroded out. Periodic rains fell percolating into voids and cavities. Minerals were moved and settled according to weight and mass (specific gravity). Atoms bonded. Mineral-rich brews began to organize into crystalline combinations according to the processes of cohesion, adhesion, and attraction of negative and positive polarities. Microscopic crystals grew larger. Some crystals displayed subtle or vivid colors depending upon various mineral combinations.

Igneous rocks produce crystals and gemstones with a legacy of heat, fire, and the incandescent birth of the Earth. Crystals and gemstones born of igneous processes will guide you through re-birthing new aspects of yourself. They will provide healing by re-generating tissue, healing organ function, and energizing your system when you are exhausted mentally, emotionally, or physically. Gemstones born of igneous processes surround you with protective energy, "burning" away fear and limitation and bringing feelings of courage and confidence.

Quartz crystals and Amethyst were born into cavities and vugs of igneous rocks. Agate, too, precipitated out of the mix and began to layer itself into colorful bands within fissures or within rock nodules and geodes, the "bubbles" of once molten rock and mud. Rocks formed of Earth's fiery processes are called "igneous."

Over time both sedimentary and igneous rock deposits were gradually buried by the accumulating dust of ages. Again, weight and pressure resulted in heat. Or, perhaps our rocks were subducted beneath miles of Earth's crust as the edges of two continental plates met and one rode up over the other. Either way they were buried deep within the Earth and subjected to massive forces that changed their configurations and altered their composition.

Time passed.

The processes of erosion and weathering, seas rising and falling to the ebb and flow of various ice ages continued, and gradually our former igneous and sedimentary rock-masses rose again to the surface of the Earth. But they were changed. They had become something else. Their journey into the depths of the Earth and back out again had transformed them into something very different than what they were originally.

Deep beneath the Earth, our sedimentary rock was subjected to even greater heat and pressure than that which originally solidified it. At vast depths intense heat caused bending, warping, and wrinkling. Our sedimentary rock was permeated with new combinations of minerals as a result of its deep-Earth sojourn.

Metamorphic rocks give birth to crystals and gemstones that contain the power of transformation. Their wisdom will take you to deep places within yourself and you will emerge with knowledge that will aid in transforming your life.

Likewise, were our igneous rocks changed and transformed. They, too, were altered by their journey deep into the abyss. What emerged in both cases was a new rock type, called, "metamorphic."

Eons beyond counting passed.

Then, one day in the far, far distant future—our own present time—a rockhound picks up a geode that has weathered out of primordial volcanic ash. She cracks it open with her rock pick and gasps at the brilliant bands of color and tiny scintillating crystals of drusy quartz exposed to light and sight for the first time in the long history of the Earth. She marvels at the beauty and magic of what lies in her hand.

Sedimentary, igneous and metamorphic rocks result from dynamic geologic processes—Earth's alchemy. Elemental processes are continually at work creating ever-evolving rock forms. This action is ongoing although from the limited perspective of a human life span we are not aware of the constantly evolving nature of the rocks beneath our feet.

Over the span of billions of years elements and minerals comprising gemstones and crystals have evolved, absorbing limitless reservoirs of wisdom and knowledge in their traverse through time. They have witnessed countless eons, eras, and ages pass by. The ceaseless parade of billions upon billions of sunsets and sunrises has passed over them in a processional blur of dark and light as they slept through countless ages.

The wisdom of the mineral world cannot be defined by the parameters of human understanding. It comprises a wider perspective incomprehensible at our present level of evolution. Yet we may tap into a narrow portion of mineral wisdom we are capable of understanding. And out of this slim fragment arises our ability to communicate with this realm.

"We are made of star stuff," said the late Carl Sagan, the eminent astronomer, writer, and creator of the celebrated TV series, "Cosmos." What is the "star stuff" of which Carl Sagan spoke? Star stuff is made of minerals and energy animated by powerful cosmic processes.

Furthermore, crystals and gemstones tell me that not only are we created of "star stuff," but that we are also evolving back to those very same stars! I cannot fully comprehend the magnitude of this concept, but on some level—a merely human one—there is a truth that resonates in my being.

It's time, now, to get acquainted with the crystals and gemstones that are used in the divination collection and learn the basic wisdom and lessons each variety wishes to share. In Chapter 7, Acquiring Crystals and Gemstones, I will give you information about the types of sources where you can acquire stones for your own divination collection.

> Perhaps the philosopher, Marsilio Ficino of Florence (1433 to 1499), intuited a similar message when he made a statement to the effect that gemstones contain the light of stars.

Gathering three each of the varieties listed in the next chapter will begin the process of opening inter-realm communication as you start assembling your collection. Spend time with each set of three stones. Hold them. Look upon them. Close your eyes and contemplate them. Feel their warmth or coolness, their subtle vibration—or inertia—as they lay in your palm. Think about them and let your mind marvel and appreciate the variety of elements and Earth processes from which these marvelous mineral beings arose. Feel gratitude and regard for the crystals and gemstones that will soon be sharing their messages and insights with you!

CHAPTER 2

The Hidden Messages Within Crystals and Gemstones

IN THIS CHAPTER YOU WILL BE INTRODUCED to the crystals and gemstones used in the divination collection as well as the basic message each has for humankind. Knowing the fundamental message of each type of gemstone is like turning the key in the lock of a long-closed door. Acquiring your divination set, handling the stones, and learning what each has to communicate will expand the channel between yourself and the mineral realm. Before long you will find that the stones are beginning to "speak" to you!

When I say that stones will "speak" I do not mean that they will make actual audible pronouncements in the same way that a person would. What does occur is that we may "see," "hear," "feel," or in some other manner intuit a stone's message via the psychic counterparts of our physical senses.

Because this book is more specifically about using crystals and gemstones for divination I have not included much information about their better-known metaphysical and healing properties. You will find limited information on the healing energies of specific stones in Chapter 10—*Water Magnetism, Dowsing, and Gemstone Elixirs.*

Our brains interpret or translate mineral realm messages and impressions in a manner we can comprehend in accordance with our sensory circuit. Thus, stones may "speak" and you may "hear" their messages but on a subliminal and psychic level rather than physically.

Furthermore, there are many wonderful books on the market that provide detailed metaphysical information on the properties of crystals and gems. Two spring readily to mind, the *Love Is in the Earth* series by Melody, and *The Crystal Bible* by Judy Hall. I have listed other books of interest in the Bibliography. Rather than try to duplicate the work of these and other superb books my goal is to present new information and revelations from the mineral realm.

Information in this chapter, specific to each type of crystal and gemstone for divination purposes, will be presented in bold and colored type to make it easier to separate from other helpful and useful details included with each stone's description.

As we learned in the previous chapter each crystal and gemstone—a combination of various elements and minerals—has been created as the result of dynamic Earth processes. As each type of crystal or gemstone is introduced I will include a little of this information. The more you become acquainted with various aspects of each stone the more you will be open to communication with it. After all, wouldn't it be easier to communicate with someone just met if you both had a little common ground first? The same is true with the mineral realm, as well.

Origins and Messages of Crystals and Gemstones

AMETHYST

Amethyst is quartz crystal that contains traces of the mineral manganese, which give it its lavender to purple coloration. Manganese is used in industry to toughen metal.

Metaphysically, manganese enhances the quality of quartz to redirect consciousness from the material to the spiritual and emotional planes. Gemstones containing manganese help us to look within. They aid in deepening meditation and initiate access to spiritual realms.

Amethyst crystals precipitate out of silica-rich liquid solutions to line cavities in rocks of igneous origin. The finest gem-grade Amethyst crystals are found deep

within the Earth, often in large geode-like structures. Part of the wisdom of Amethyst is that of diving deeply past the consciousness to the subconscious and beyond—right to the spiritual plane!

All quartz crystals, Amethyst included, are composed mostly of silica, one of the most abundant minerals on Earth, superseded only by feldspar. For the divination collection, Amethyst as crystal points or tumble polished nodules, faceted gems, or cabochons may be used. You may also use "Chevron" Amethyst with its interesting arrow-shaped bands of white and lavender.

The primary mineral message associated with Amethyst, whether in the form of crystals, polished cabochons, or tumble polished nodules always regards spiritual matters and issues. When drawn by a querist (one who is receiving a reading)—or avoided—it speaks of an interest in, a need for—or avoidance of—introducing a spiritual facet into one's life.

Depending upon which stones Amethyst is situated with in a reading, its general meaning will be clarified or altered.

> The Life Lesson of Amethyst is, "There is no life without spirit." Life would be extremely one-dimensional without a spiritual element. It is the spiritual component that adds meaning, hope, graciousness and beauty to life.

Amethyst, drawn during the health portion of a reading, represents the need to integrate a spiritual aspect into one's life.

Substitutes: Lavender Sugilite may substitute for amethyst in the readings.

AMEGREEN/AMETRINE

Two similar stones, the "fraternal, but not identical, twins" of the mineral world carry nearly twin messages! Both are of igneous origin.

Acquire whichever comes to you first as long as the two colors that compose each are sharply visible. Some Ametrine is nearly indistinguishable from Amethyst as the Citrine band is almost non-existent.

20 CRYSTAL AND GEMSTONE DIVINATION

Amegreen

If you choose to use Ametrine be sure that the Citrine band is easily visible. These specimens of Ametrine show poor Citrine coloration and would easily be mistaken for tumble polished Amethyst Crystals.

Amegreen is an Amethyst and Green Quartz combination. Either Amegreen or Ametrine may be used in the divination collection. Both combine the "spiritual" message of Amethyst with the "abundance" and "new beginning" messages of Citrine and Green Quartz. Thus, Amegreen's (and Ametrine's) message is about transformation on spiritual and physical levels. Amegreen is most often found as tumble polished nodules and natural crystals. Ametrine is found as tumble polished nodules and natural crystals, but be sure the Citrine band is easily distinguishable.

These gemstones are all about transformation when drawn during a reading. Symbolically their message can be described as rising Kundalini energy, the alchemical crucible, or the Cauldron of Transformation. They both speak to the soul of deep or radical transformation that affects one on all levels!

Where Citrine's or Green Quartz' messages are of elective or natural change, when combined with Amethyst the messages are of major transformation—transformation that may be life or consciousness altering, often coming unbidden, but in a BIG way.

Both of these stones can herald a physical illness or major life-trial that will awaken one from apathy or monotony to a discovery of what truly has meaning. On the positive side, these gemstones may herald sudden healing from a chronic malady,

THE HIDDEN MESSAGES WITHIN CRYSTALS AND GEMSTONES

a remission of life-threatening illness, or some major course change in one's life. The querist who selects one of these is on the cusp of BIG change!

> The Life Lesson of Amegreen/Ametrine is, "Be ready to leap empty-handed into uncharted territory!"

These stones represent the glands, the chakras (energy vortexes in the body), and the aura in a health reading.

Amegreen or Ametrine, while being gemstones of uncommon energy, are quite readily available.

Substitutes: You can substitute Olivine if necessary.

APACHE TEAR

This translucent, tawny stone is a type of high-vibrational volcanic glass called obsidian. It is formed when globules of silica-rich, superheated lava are extruded and rapidly cooled.

Our ancient ancestors flaked and used obsidian to create knives and arrowheads for both hunting and protection. When flaked, obsidian has an edge comparable to the sharpest surgical scalpel. Hence, obsidian is used metaphysically for protection of both the physical and spiritual surroundings. Its energy "slices through" negativity.

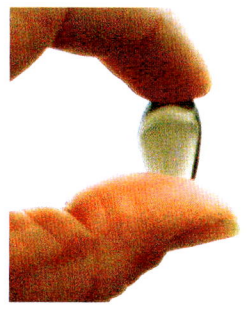

When polished, Black Obsidian is extremely shiny. Shamans, diviners and oracles have long used it to peer into astral planes as well as to witness future events.

Apache Tear is said to be the solidified tears of Native American women and women worldwide mourning the loss of warriors, husbands, children, and culture to war and pestilence. Tumble polished or natural nodules are the usual forms used in the readings.

In a crystal and gemstone reading, Apache Tear's message is a warning that feelings of despair, hopelessness, or emptiness are either present or soon will be. Apache Tear advises that these feeling are present, or will be, and to take whatever steps are necessary to try to alleviate these feelings. This gemstone warns that if left un-addressed or unhealed these feelings may lead to withdrawal, and at worst, to suicidal thoughts and impulses.

The message of this stone may seem negative but ultimately leads to healing. Apache Tear may also indicate a "no" answer to a question. It can assert that a direction the querist is considering will have negative effects or that a particular situation, or relationship, should be avoided as it will lead to sadness or ultimate misery.

The Life Lesson of Apache Tear is, "Why me."

In the health portion of a reading Apache Tear represents a warning so that a situation may be avoided or anticipated and thereby ameliorated. Health-wise Apache Tear advises that there is a nutritional lack or deficiency on some level or that depression is affecting physical health.

Substitutes: You may use tumble polished Black Obsidian or Tektite—meteoric glass —if you cannot find Apache Tear.

AQUAMARINE

This translucent gemstone is usually light blue, bluish-green, to pale green in color. Aquamarine is a type of beryl. As such it is one of the hardest gemstones approaching closely to diamond in hardness. While diamonds are considered to have a rating of "10" on a Mohs hardness scale (a functional means used to determine relative hardness in minerals), Aquamarine comes in at around "7.5 to 8." Aquamarine precipitates out of

THE HIDDEN MESSAGES WITHIN CRYSTALS AND GEMSTONES

liquids rich in beryllium, aluminum, and silica. The mineral, aluminum, has a resonance with Divine Mind and the human mind. However, accumulation of aluminum in its refined form in brain tissue is thought to be one of the factors implicated in causing Alzheimer's disease.

"Mind" and "brain" are two somewhat related but different concepts! Aluminum, in its natural, unrefined state, seems to conduct false concepts and limiting beliefs into awareness so they may be recognized and eliminated.

Beryllium, another element in Aquamarine, has a "distilling" quality enabling one to isolate rational, linear thought from confused and turbulent emotions, thereby clarifying the thought processes and aiding in problem solving.

Aquamarine is born in hydrothermal veins within igneous and sometimes metamorphic rock. Tumble polished nodules are the commonest forms on the market.

The primary message of Aquamarine is that of ideas, logic, and the rational application of the creative process. It speaks to us of common sense, education, mind, and intellect. Aquamarine advises us to "think clearly and carefully" about an issue. In circumstances where emotions run high, Aquamarine cautions not to lose one's ability to think clearly.

The Life Lesson of Aquamarine is, "Be prepared." This may be accomplished by conceiving a plan or strategy before embarking on any endeavor.

In the health portion of a reading this stone represents the head and brain. It may indicate a tendency toward stress headaches, migraines, or some other illness regarding the head, jaw, and facial area, or an inability to sleep in a restful manner.

Substitutes: For use in the readings, Prehnite with a similar primary message and Life Message may be used. Blue Aventurine may also be substituted for Aquamarine.

BLOODSTONE

Bloodstone is considered to be a semi-precious, microcrystalline quartz gemstone. Bloodstone—as are most Agates—is formed by precipitation of silica-rich liquid into cavities of igneous rock. Bloodstone is usually opaque, dark green in color overall, with flecks, spots, or bands of red, hence the appellation "Bloodstone." Occasionally, other colors such as white or yellow will occur within the dominant green and lesser red hues.

Bloodstone's energy is about tact and compromise. It teaches us a tactful response or dignified withdrawal by saying what needs expressing but keeping a rein on anger, recrimination, and the desire to verbally wound another during a disagreement. Fear often lies at the root of uncontrolled or flash-point anger.

Bloodstone is the gemstone to wear or carry for diplomats and debaters for it teaches us that we can make our point without the need to demean or inflict verbal abuse on another. Look for tumble polished nodules, small wands, or cabochons.

In the readings, Bloodstone speaks to us of loving relationships that may be marred or damaged by harsh words, criticism, misunderstanding, or resentment. Bloodstone teaches us that tact and consideration can overcome issues and disagreements and important points of view may be made diplomatically and with grace and compassion.

In the health portion of the readings, Bloodstone "represents" emotional and physical disease and counsels moderation in all things.

> The Life Lesson of Bloodstone is, "You are safe."

Substitutes: Dark Green Agate or any combination of red and green, or red and black, or red and mauve colors may be substituted.

THE HIDDEN MESSAGES WITHIN CRYSTALS AND GEMSTONES   25

BLUE LACE AGATE

Blue Lace Agate is born of silica-rich precipitate into cavities in igneous rocks. Its soft blue color indicates that it gently burns away obstacles to positive interaction. This gemstone is most commonly marketed as tumble polished nodules.

In a reading Blue Lace Agate indicates that a boy or male is being brought to the attention of the querist. This may mean that a son, nephew, brother, father, husband, or male lover is of concern or interest in the life of the querist. Look to surrounding stones to better define the relationship.

Early springtime may be indicated by Blue Lace Agate if timing is an important factor in a reading.

The Life Lesson of Blue Lace Agate is, "Soar." This stone advises us to be all that we can be! Blue Lace Agate represents the throat and communication.

Substitutes: Any light blue Agate or Chalcedony may be substituted for Blue Lace Agate in the readings.

CARNELIAN

Carnelian is an orange or reddish form of Chalcedony and originates in low-temperature silica-rich precipitates in seams or cavities of igneous rocks. It is most often translucent and sometimes displays bands of orange-red or cream colors. The predominantly orangey-red color of Carnelian is due to traces of hematite and limonite (iron oxides) entering the precipitate.

The energy of iron imbues this gemstone with the attributes of will and determination. In ancient days, Carnelian was worn to dispel fear and improve amplitude and vigor of the voice. Those wanting to improve their station in life through schooling or apprenticeship wore Carnelian. It is still worn today in the Middle East to bring luck and dispel negative emotions, such as envy. Tumble polished nodules, cabochons, and beads are the forms most commonly found.

Used in readings, Carnelian speaks particularly to those who are or should be seeking their muse...especially in creative outlets such as hobbies and the arts, such as theatre, writing, music, painting, fashion, design, and sculpture. Carnelian advises one to hone inherent talents and amplify them through learning and practice. This stone also has a message for those who are students, or undergoing apprenticeship, learning a trade, or contemplating turning a hobby or creative outlet into a business enterprise, especially when paired with Citrine in a layout.

The Life Lesson of Carnelian is, "Find your Muse."

In the health portion of the readings, Carnelian represents the pancreas.

Substitutes: Carnelian is a commonly found gemstone and no substitute should be needed.

CITRINE

Citrine is quartz crystal with traces of colloidal iron hydrates that give it a yellow to brownish hue. Citrine is born of silica-rich precipitate in cavities in igneous rock.

The Romans prized Citrine for use as an engraved gem for rings and brooches. This stone has the power to cleanse the atmosphere of negative vibrations and is worn as a protective amulet. Citrine was once used in magic spells to manifest new beginnings and dispel old energy.

Citrine may be used in either its crystalline form or as tumble polished nodules in the divination collection.

Citrine's message is one of new cycles, new beginnings, and starting fresh or seeing things from a new, positive perspective. Seeing Citrine in a reading indicates the beginning of a new project or a new start or change in some phase of life. The message of this stone is positive and generally indicates that the new cycle will be successful unless paired with stones carrying a negative message.

The Life Lesson of Citrine is, "Start something new."

In the health portion of the reading this stone represents the joints of the body and may indicate potential or actual arthritic and rheumatic conditions. It may also imply that flexibility is needed in the "figurative" sense, as well.

Substitutes: Citrine is very easy to find and should need no substitute.

CRAZY LACE AGATE

Crazy Lace Agate, another silica-rich precipitate of igneous origin, is usually opaque to translucent, white or cream in color with patterns and plumes of brown, rust, pink, gray, and orange. The patterns running through this stone look like routes on an Atlas or map —perhaps "a road less traveled"—that leads one to a new place!

Crazy Lace Agate displays these markings to speak to humankind of physical movement and change of scene. The specific type of movement spoken of is travel to someplace new, not as a vacation, but to live—as in immigration or relocation. Look for tumble polished nodules and cabochons.

Crazy Lace Agate's message is one of relocation...moving one's household. A change of household may constitute buying or renting a new home or relocation due to marriage or job change. Occasionally, Crazy Lace Agate refers to remodeling or redecorating an existing home, or a strong desire to move but not presently having the means to do so.

The Life Lesson of Crazy Lace Agate is, "Home is where the heart is."

In the health portion of a reading, this gemstone represents the skin, skin conditions, or the need to care for the skin in some way.

Substitutes: Crazy Lace Agate may be substituted by Picture Agate, or by any "Plume" or "Flame" Agate.

DALMATIAN AGATE

Dalmatian Agate is a silica-rich precipitate and with a little imagination, when held at a distance, may appear similar to letters or hieroglyphs of text and spots of ink on parchment paper. This appearance suggests its message to us of legal, binding agreements. It speaks of contracts, wills, legal issues, licensing, permits, law suits, marriage, divorce, traffic tickets, taxes ...anything of a legal or magisterial nature or pertaining to laws and justice. Look for tumble polished nodules.

In the crystal and gemstone readings this stone suggests that a legal issue of some type is looming for the querist.

The Life Lesson of Dalmatian Agate is, "Render unto Caesar."

In the health portion of the reading it represents muscle tissue and meat in the diet.

Substitutes: Gray or Black Banded Agate, Spotted Agate, or Banded Onyx of similar colors may substitute for this stone.

FLUORITE

Fluorite occurs as cubic crystals and masses. It comes in a variety of colors such as yellow, white, pink, green, lavender and purple. It may be composed of intermixed bands of many of these colors.

Fluorite is born out of medium and high-temperature hydrothermal veins in igneous rock. Occasionally fluorite may be introduced into sedimentary rock by precipitate originating out of igneous rock.

Fluorite is a combination of calcium and fluorine compounds. It is used industrially as a flux in the manufacture of ceramic glazes and steel. It is also used to make high-quality optics.

This gemstone is often marketed in the form of "octahedrons." An octahedron is created when cubic fluorite is struck so that it breaks, or "cleaves" along a plane of weakness of the molecules forming its cubic crystals.

Octahedrons look like two four-sided pyramids that have been stuck together at their bases. Natural cubic fluorite crystals, pieces cut to resemble crystal points, octahedrons, or tumble polished nodules may be used in the divination collection. Octahedrons and tumble polished nodules are forms commonly found at gem shows, rock shops, and New Age stores.

The message of Fluorite relates to a specialized craft, expertise, or skill. Where Carnelian spoke of apprenticeship and finding one's muse, this stone speaks of the ability to take a well-honed skill or craft and market it, not only to make money, but also to serve others.

As an example, Fluorite might be a stone that would attract someone who is not only interested in theater, but who is actually an actor. It may draw someone who not only has an interest in writing but also makes income from writing. It might call to one who has efficiently organized her home, and then goes on to create a business where she advises others on how to de-clutter and organize their own homes.

Fluorite is a stone that has a message for those who have become educated in, or honed a skill or craft to the point of proficiency and expertise. This gemstone attracts those on the forefront of their profession who are using their craft to discover new frontiers, such as a professors, professional people, doctors, or scientists.

The Life Lesson of Fluorite is, "Work is Spirit made manifest."

It represents the teeth and mouth.

Substitutes: Fluorite is easily found wherever crystals and gemstones are sold. Calcite in blue, green, or pink may be substituted.

FOSSILIZED DINOSAUR BONE

This gemstone-fossil is formed of silica that has percolated into the interstices of dinosaur bone replacing the original organic matter while maintaining the structural appearance of both cells and tissue. Fossilized Dinosaur Bone is identified as black or brown in color, often with circular red or pink patterns caused by silica replacement of the blood vessels and marrow. These circular patterns speak to us of emblems, tokens, medals and merit. This gemstone may also be called "Leopard Skin" Agate. Tumble polished nodules are the commonest forms on the market.

Due to the replacement of original dinosaur tissue with something else, in this case silica, the message of this stone is of that which forms the framework— or bones—of how we meet our basic life needs—food and shelter.

For non-industrial cultures Dinosaur Bone might describe a shift or deviation in the hunting or gathering possibilities such as movement of game or increase or failure in crops. Perhaps it might hint at some change having to do with one's trade or craft that provides for one's basic physical needs. In our culture this stone describes changes in career, profession, trade, or job as that is how most of us acquire food, shelter, and luxuries.

When selected as part of a reading, Fossilized Dinosaur Bone tells us that the querist is about to have a change in his or her work situation such as looking for and finding a job, or may be getting ready to change jobs or receive a promotion. This stone can indicate an increase in money, but it is money that comes from merit, or earning power, rather than as a gift.

The Life Lesson of Fossilized Dinosaur Bone is,
"Betterment of circumstances."

During the health portion of the reading Fossilized Dinosaur Bone represents the bone marrow, and digestion as related to blood production within the marrow.

Substitutes: Petrified Wood, "Orbicular Agate," and "Orbicular Jasper" may be substituted for this gemstone. The word "orbicular" denotes "ring" or "disk-shaped."

GIRASOL

Girasol is a form of watery-clear Opal, sometimes with a faint bluish hue. It contains no fire and is a type of "amorphous" silica—meaning that it is a non-crystalline form of silica. Opal of any type is a silica-precipitate that retains water within its structure. It is born of fiery and sedimentary processes and its overall energy is quite watery, much more so than Quartz Crystal. Because Girasol has no fire, as do many of the gem-quality opals, its price is quite reasonable.

Girasol has a protective, fluid energy that gently penetrates to and fiercely protects and shields that part of each of us that houses our deepest, most sensitive feelings.

The message of Girasol speaks directly to the sensitive, emotional part of ourselves we keep hidden and protected because of fears of rejection or potential hurt. Those that have been rejected or betrayed by a parent or some other important figure in their lives may have a reservoir of feelings they protect from exposure due to distrust or fear of being hurt again.

When looking for Girasol, look for natural pieces and tumble polished nodules.

Girasol speaks about sensitive, protected emotions. It tells us to share our important feelings with those we love. This stone has another message and that is to take care against being "over sensitive" to perceived slights. Girasol advises us not to look for insults where none were intended and to be less thin-skinned.

The Life Lesson of Girasol is, "I feel."

In the health portion of this reading, this gemstone represents the need of water in ones environment, the need to drink more water, and specifically speaks about the lymphatic system.

Substitutes: Lavender Jade or translucent Lavender Chalcedony may be used as substitutes for Girasol. Other types of common Opal (without fire) may be substituted, as well.

HEMATITE

Hematite (iron oxide) is an iron ore often carved into cabochons and beads. It takes a high polish and is silvery or charcoal-gray in color. It feels heavy for its size due to its 70% iron content. Hematite is the true "blood stone" of the ancients. This silvery-gray mineral when drawn across unglazed tile leaves a red streak. When ground and polished it "bleeds" ochre red. The most commonly found forms are as tumble polished nodules and beads.

Hematite's message speaks to us of our own Iron Age and the skills we applied to the forming of metals and other natural materials into tools and goods. This stone, when drawn during a reading, reveals that the querist holds a reverence for the past, remembering ones roots, origins, and culture.

A querist drawing this stone likely has an interest in ancestral handcrafts such as spinning, weaving, dyeing, ironwork, candle and soap making, and so on. Hematite attracts those with professions dependent upon a "use of the hands" or who choose manual processes over those performed by machines. People who have an affinity to a certain historical time period, such as the civil war, gold rush, or pioneering eras, are drawn to this stone as are hunters, fishermen, and farmers.

The Life Lesson of Hematite is, "Where there's a will, there's a way.

Hematite represents the blood and iron in the diet. Selected during a health reading this stone suggests the inclusion of mineral-iron from the ingestion of iron-rich foods, using a cast iron pan to cook with, and bringing "iron' will to your endeavors. This stone however, does not counsel the ingestion of iron supplements in pill form.

Substitutes: Lodestone (a magnetic form of iron ore) may be substituted for Hematite.

LABRADORITE

Either the "white" or more common "dark" form may be used in the divination collection. Both types of Labradorite display blue iridescence. Labradorite is composed of calcium, sodium, and aluminum-silicate and is born out of the fire of volcanic activity, as well as to those metamorphic processes occurring to igneous rocks.

This gemstone is a type of feldspar, which is the most common mineral on the planet closely followed by silica. Industrially, Labradorite is used in ceramics and glazes, and in manufacturing methods that use fire as part of production. Labradorite occurs in a few U.S. and Canadian areas, but most deposits are overseas. Therefore, Labradorite has much to relate regarding travel and messages that move over water (represented by its blue iridescence) and over long distance.

This gemstone is marketed as "rough," tumble polished nodules, and cabochons.

Labradorite speaks to us of news coming in, news from a distance or news from someone unknown to the querist. It may also indicate travel when selected during a reading.

The electric-blue fire of Labradorite symbolizes transmission of news, usually via phone, telegraph, computer, or other electronic means, although news could come in letter or printed form. News may also travel from one person to another in the way that gossip does. The blue fire of this stone can indicate water and may mean that travel may be over or near water.

> The Life Lesson of Laboradite is, "Tidings are heading your way."

In the healing portion of the reading this stone represents the need for "time out" by taking a vacation, a day trip, or just getting away from the house or job.

Substitutes: Labradorite is easily found.

LEPIDOLITE

Lepidolite is lavender in color. It is composed of hydrous potassium, lithium, and aluminum silicate. Lepidolite is often the matrix, or mother material, in which pink tourmaline grows. Lepidolite with or without small crystals of pink tourmaline may be used in the readings.

Lepidolite is an ore of the mineral, lithium. It belongs to the mica group of minerals meaning that its crystals form in platelets. It has the ability to calm and soothe. Lepidolite is born of igneous processes, however, lithium adds calming qualities not inherent to most igneous rocks. Look for "rough" or tumble polished nodules.

In the readings Lepidolite may indicate something or someone from the past, an old person, a tradition, or custom. It warns of outworn modes of behavior or habits that should be left behind. It may also refer to the "wintertime" of the year.

The Life Lesson of Lepidolite is, "Know when to let go."

Lepidolite represents the ability to let go of what no longer serves.

Substitutes: Rubellite (reddish-pink) Tourmaline, Pink Tourmaline, or mottled Lavender Agate may substitute for Lepidolite.

LINED AGATE

When assembling your divination set, look for beige, cream, or greenish to brown Agate having lines or bands. This gemstone is sometimes marketed as "Picasso Stone." The pattern on this Agate suggests "disturbance." Lined Agate is opaque. It is formed in the same way as other Agates out of silica-rich precipitates in igneous rocks.

Lined Agate is most commonly marketed as tumble polished nodules, beads, or cabochons.

This stone's message to human kind may seem negative as it speaks of conflict within oneself and with others. Its purpose is to awaken a querist to conflicts so that they may be worked through so resolution can begin. When you see this stone in a reading there is conflict with others, with self, or with life situations. Lined Agate also warns that conflict of some type is on the horizon. This gemstone gives a negative, or "no" answer to a question. Note what stones are in proximity. Further information will be revealed!

**The Life Lesson of Lined Agate is,
"There is nothing to fear but fear itself."**

Fear sometimes resides behind conflict of any type. Conflict is an outward expression of one's own fears or those of others.

In the healing portion of the reading, Lined Agate represents the digestive tract, especially the process of digestion. This gemstone counsels introducing bitter greens into the diet in the form of collards, the greens of mustard, turnip, or dandelions, broccoli, watercress, and parsley. It recommends herbal infusions of dandelion leaf and root, nettle, and peppermint.

Substitutes: Any color of lined, striped, banded, or patterned Agate or Jasper may substitute.

MAGNESITE

Magnesite is a non-crystalline opaque stone composed of magnesium, carbon, and oxygen. It arises out of metamorphic processes. Magnesite is usually white or cream in color with veins of brown, gray or black magnesium. This stone may be smooth and waxy in appearance or "bubbly." Magnesite is marketed as tumble polished nodules or "rough" nuggets and is sometimes called "Howlite."

In a gemstone reading this stone's message is one of fate and karma and of heavenly grace.

The Life Lesson of Magnesite is, "Harm none, for Love is the Law."

In the health portion of the readings, Magnesite represents karmic (or genetic) issues that may be affecting one's life and health.

Substitutes: Magnesite may be substituted by Dolomite, which is mineralogically similar and carries a related message. Dolomite often forms in cubic crystals and is usually pale pink. Green or yellow-green Turquoise may also substitute.

MALACHITE

Malachite is found in the oxidation zone of copper deposits and belongs to the family of minerals called "carbonates." Carbonates form when sets of complex conditions are just right. Carbon dioxide from the atmosphere, hydrogen ions from water, and bicarbonate ions all bond. To this mix, precise conditions of pressure, temperature and concentration of elements must occur for the formation of the triangular ions that underlie the structure of this family of minerals.

Triangular ions of the carbonate family are bound together by ions of copper—two ions in the case of Malachite, three ions for Azurite—generating a type of energy with the ability to aid humankind and the planet to manifest forms on all levels.

Copper ore was one of the first metals (tin in other areas) liquefied out of ore and poured into molds to make tools, weapons and mirrors. How did early humans learn to heat stones to high enough temperatures to liquefy and extract the metal within?

We are told that this was a purely accidental process discovered around the campfire when superheated Malachite or Azurite dribbled out liquid copper. Maybe. Maybe not. In most cases campfires alone are not hot enough to melt the metal out of rock. A billows is needed to create heat sufficient to do the job.

Remember, however, that our ancient ancestors communicated with crystals and gemstones. The processes of metalworking were perhaps an accidental process but more likely occurred as the result of communication between humankind and the mineral realm!

When solid and of gem quality, Malachite is used in jewelry. This gemstone often forms with Azurite, a blue-green copper mineral that, when of gem grade, is also made into jewelry.

Weapons and mirrors—the first for protection and hunting, the other to see one's reflection—and always, Malachite was worn to adorn the body and for its magical powers. Malachite was a gemstone worn by children in ancient times to protect them from kidnapping.

Protective energy permeates Malachite. Look for solid (not grainy), tumble polished nodules, beads, and cabochons when assembling your divination set.

In a reading, drawing Malachite indicates that the querist should take measures to protect him- or herself, a family member, or property. Lock your home, your garage, your car. Malachite warns that a situation is arising where caution or safety is needed. Drawing more than one may indicate that the querist has a desire to be protected or may be a warning that danger, theft, or accident are imminent.

> The Life Lesson of Malachite is, "Love, Strength, and Beauty." Love, strength, and beauty were the attributes of Hathor, an Egyptian goddess, whose Roman and Greek equivalents were Venus and Aphrodite. Temples to Hathor were often erected near or within Egyptian copper mines, as she was the patron goddess of miners. Hathor was also divine protectress of children and women in childbirth.

In a health reading Malachite represents the immune system and advises that steps be taken to strengthen immunity.

Substitutes: Azurite may be substituted for Malachite in the gemstone readings.

MOONSTONE

Moonstone is a type of feldspar, called Albite, originating out of igneous rock. Moonstone is rich in aluminum, sodium, silica, and calcium. Another type of Moonstone (Adularia) is rich in potassium instead of calcium. Either type may be used in the divination collection.

Translucence and sheen makes this stone desirable as jewelry. Any color, or color combination, or pattern of Moonstone may be used.

As part of the feldspar group of minerals, Moonstone is very closely related to Labradorite. Look for small spheres, beads, cabochons, or tumble polished nodules.

Moonstone has long been believed to be a "woman's" stone and with good reason. Our ancestors intuited that the energy of women, the Moon, and this gemstone were in harmony.

Therefore, in the gemstone readings, Moonstone speaks about women. When Moonstone is drawn as part of a reading a querist may be assured that this gemstone is speaking about a girl or woman. This would be a female (mother, wife, sister, friend, mentor, or lover) in the life of the querist. Moonstone may also indicate time as late spring into summer.

> **The Life Lesson of Amethyst is, "Attitude is everything."**

Moonstone is serene but has another side, a sassy, feminine "you go Girl" energy that may be tapped into. Although the Moon is far distant from our planet, it still regulates the tides of mighty oceans as well as women's inner tides.

Moonstone has a message for young women living in a society that still carries antiquated messages labeling women as an inferior gender. Moonstone emphatically states that the feminine sex is not inferior! Within Moonstone lies the energy of strength and will. Some men tend to equate physical strength with dominance and superiority. Yet, as humankind evolves in our modern world, this type of "power-over" forceful, physical dominance has given way to stamina, mental abilities, and determination. Women have these qualities in abundance. Qualities other than physical strength, in most cases, determine success and wealth in our present stage of evolution.

Moonstone represents rest, serenity, and the female organs.

Substitutes: Moonstone is easily found and needs no substitutes.

MOSS AGATE

Moss Agate may be translucent or opaque. The overall coloration is usually translucent to opaque-white with inclusions of green "moss." The moss is actually composed of dendrites of manganese. Moss Agate may also show reverse coloration and be predominantly green with milky white inclusions.

Moss Agate reminds me of what the Earth looks like as seen from outer space. One can imagine its white coloration as wispy, white clouds revealing green continents below. Moss Agate suggests peace and quietude although it is born of igneous processes. The mineral, manganese (as oxides of pyrolusite and psilomelane) softens and redirects much of the igneous energy.

Moss Agate expresses energy in much the same way that a walk in natural surroundings helps settle turbulent emotions. This gemstone is usually sold as tumble polished nodules and cabochons.

Moss Agate's message is one of connection with Nature and the Earth. This stone's coloration speaks to us of trees, green and growing things, and the abundance of the soil upon which we live and have our sustenance. This stone will resonate with those who love the outdoors, whether through sports, gardening, or other outdoor activity.

The Life Lesson of Moss Agate is, "Care of the Earth."

Moss Agate represents the need for connection with the Earth through some type of outdoor activity where one can commune with Nature. Picnicking, outdoor photography, yoga, jogging, walking your dog or riding, camping, fishing, hiking, golf, or sitting under a tree...something where you get out and enjoy sky, wind, soil, plants, animals, birds. This gemstone's message is especially relevant today because too many of us spend most of our life indoors. This stone tells us that we must get out and expose ourselves to the healing energies of Nature, the energies of Sun, Wind, Water, and Earth.

In the health part of a reading this gemstone represents the lower legs and feet. Because feet symbolize our ability to understand issues, this gemstone may be advising a querist that there is something he or she is failing to understand that may be having an influence regarding a health issue.

Substitutes: Any Agate with green (or brown) and white color combinations may be used to substitute for Moss Agate.

PINK AVENTURINE

Pink Aventurine, a type of cryptocrystalline quartz with inclusions of sparkling scales of mica, is born of silica-rich precipitate in igneous rocks. The inclusions of mica aid one in seeing all sides of a situation—something that a wise mentor or leader will gently aid one to do.

Pink Aventurine speaks to us of elders, mentors, parents, sometimes spirit guides, angels, and totem spirits—those who, whether of the physical realm or the spiritual, want to help and guide us. Look for this gemstone as tumble polished nodules or small spheres or "wands."

When Pink Aventurine is selected during a reading the querist is soon to receive helpful advice, illumination on some problem, or wisdom from someone in authority, a wise person, or even a spiritual being. This gemstone may also counsel a querist to seek such advice.

The Life Lesson of Pink Aventurine is, "Seek and you shall find.

In the health portion of the reading, Pink Aventurine represents the liver.

Substitutes: Pink or Mauve Agate, or a combination of Agate in pink and gray may substitute for Pink Aventurine. Mauve, pink, or Gray Chalcedony or Chert may also be substituted.

PYRITE

Pyrite is composed of iron sulfides and forms in hydrothermal veins. It is a stone to wear when you find yourself in "hot water!" Its mineral wisdom will help you extricate yourself from difficult situations or avoid them altogether.

Pyrite is metallic, brassy-gold in color and tends to form in cubic crystals. It has been mistaken for gold and has earned the name "fools gold." Unlike gold which is relatively soft and malleable and can be stretched and flattened without shattering, Pyrite is hard and brittle. It is found near streams and creeks and has an affinity for water and therefore is sometimes used to heal inflammation. It occasionally occurs in deposits of fluorite. This combination makes a striking and powerful jewelry piece. The mineral-marriage of Pyrite and Fluorite is harmonious and symbiotic.

Pyrite is often found in and around the same mineral deposits that contain gold. It is usually marketed as small, cubic clusters, as large individual cubes, or as tumble polished "nuggets."

Pyrite's message is one of falsehood, trickery, deception, and enmity. It advises one to investigate and take care before agreeing to something or getting involved.

"Beware" is the primary message of Pyrite. Sometimes if something looks too good to be true, it's probably untrue.

Pyrite may attract a querist who has recently suffered betrayal or deception of some type. This stone may warn that such lies in the near future and to maintain awareness.

When this stone is drawn take particular care to look beyond outer appearances, peer behind the scenes, and investigate all aspects carefully and fully before committing oneself, time, or money to an idea, opportunity, or relationship. Pyrite always indicates some type of falsehood whether as lies, misrepresentation, or misconduct. It may also caution that some important detail has been overlooked. A spurious or deceptive relationship and enmity are deeper implications of the message of Pyrite. While this stone's message may seem negative, the wisdom behind it is one of resolution. This gemstone brings the issue of falsity, enmity, and deceptive relationships to the surface where they may be brought to awareness and dealt with.

Unlike Bloodstone whose meaning is of loving relationships that have negative aspects, Pyrite speaks of relationships that should end or should not be entered into. Pyrite may warn that trouble and trickery surrounds a relationship or that an enemy lurks on the horizon about to be revealed.

>The Life Lesson of Pyrite is, "Look before you leap."

In a health reading this gemstone represents the stomach and counsels against overeating, compulsive eating, and proactive care of the digestive processes. It may warn of indigestion, acid reflux, ulcers, etc. Take care with the diet. Be aware of what you put into your body. Limit the intake of "fake" or "junk" foods. Be moderate in the use of alcohol and addictive foods or drugs. Foods that have been overly adulterated with fat, sugar, salt, or are synthetic, irradiated, or with man-made chemicals added are indicated.

Substitutes: Pyrite is easily found and needs no substitute.

QUARTZ CRYSTAL

Clear Quartz Crystals are composed primarily of silica and form in cavities of igneous rocks. As the rocks weather and erode, quartz crystals may be found in loose deposits in the Earth where the rocks once existed. They may also be found downhill of their original host or "mother" rock, after weathering out of fissures.

Quartz Crystals have the ability to store and transmit information because of the purity of their silica content. When quartz is cut along a precise angle to its axis it is capable of transmitting a weak electrical charge.

THE HIDDEN MESSAGES WITHIN CRYSTALS AND GEMSTONES

This makes quartz useful for transmitting equipment such as radio, television, and radar. Quartz also transmits wavelengths of light better than glass. It can split white light into its rainbow components. The ability of quartz to transmit energy of various types makes it a valuable meditation and scrying or "gazing" stone. In ancient times Quartz Crystal was believed to be ice that had turned to stone!

Look for mini-crystal points when assembling your divination set.

Quartz Crystals are born of igneous rocks. Therefore their message to us in the readings is that of energy, strength, vitality and willpower. They speak of animation and our own inner strength that has the power to bring success. When a querist selects a Quartz Crystal it may be that he or she is unsure that efforts will result in success. The message of Quartz Crystal is that the querist does indeed have the resources to succeed if he or she believes in, and applies, oneself. Drawing this crystal gives the querist assurance of a positive, successful outcome and a "yes" answer to a question despite doubts to the contrary.

When more than one Quartz Crystal is selected—especially if laid down pointing in the same direction—the message is that of forward movement and putting plans into action. The querist is being advised that energy is now right for taking action or pursuing the course in question. If not pointing the same way, two or more Quartz Crystal may be indicating that the querist needs to simplify her goal or perhaps has too many "irons in the fire."

In the health portion of a reading Quartz Crystal represents the spine, lower back, connecting nerves (ganglia), and skeleton.

> The Life Lesson of Quartz Crystal is, "Belief in the strength of self."
> This stone teaches that despite outside influences your own innate
> ability is what will enable you to make your dreams a reality.

Substitutions: Quartz Crystal is common and easy to find and I recommend the natural crystal form so as not to confuse this stone with Girasol. However, tumble polished Quartz Crystal or cabochons containing filaments of Rutile (Rutilated Quartz) may be substituted for Quartz Crystal. Rutilated Quartz carries the same message as Quartz Crystal while placing slightly more emphasis on the "go for it" aspect of the message of Quartz Crystal.

RED JASPER

Red Jasper is an opaque form of crypto-crystalline quartz usually red-orange to red in color. Unlike Carnelian, Red Jasper is opaque, rather than translucent. Hematite (iron oxide) gives this gemstone its reddish color and power of attraction. It works on energetic levels similar to how iron filings are drawn to a magnet. This stone resonates with Nature's procreative potency!

Red Jasper has a message for humankind about passionate love and relationships! The type of love Jasper communicates is that of sexual passion between loving couples. Physical attraction is one of the important bonding components of Jasper-love.

Lovers, or those seeking love, will want to wear or carry Red Jasper due to its qualities of attraction. Red Jasper will infuse your aura with the orange light-wave (as will Carnelian) that helps make one attractive to potential love interests. The energy of Red Jasper also brings respect and unity between people and a desire to nurture and care for one another. Wearing Red Jasper is said to prolong and enhance sexual pleasure. This gemstone is most commonly found on the market as tumble polished nodules, beads, and cabochons.

The Life Lesson of Red Jasper is, "Love makes the world go round."

In the readings Red Jasper communicates love and passion. Red Jasper speaks of love usually with an element of physical attraction and expression.

In the health portion of the readings, Red Jasper represents sexual expression, rather than potency or fertility, in both men and women.

Substitutes: Commonly found, Red Jasper needs no substitute.

RED TIGER EYE

Tiger Eye and Red Tiger Eye are both a form of crystalline quartz with inclusions of asbestos fibers. Asbestos is a fibrous silicate known for its heat resistance and is also considered toxic when isolated. It is not toxic to handle or make tinctures with gemstones such as Tiger Eye or Serpentine as the asbestos is rendered inert by its encapsulation by silica.

Red Tiger Eye is formed when golden Tiger Eye is heated either naturally or artificially. You could say that Red Tiger Eye is golden Tiger Eye on steroids!

Red Tiger Eye has a message to relate to humankind regarding perfection. In a reading this stone will attract those to whom perfection and idealism rate highly—sometimes to their detriment—as in the case of expecting too much of oneself or others.

Red Tiger Eye is the gemstone for those who've taken multitasking to the extreme, who are too much on the go, or tend to over schedule. Red Tiger Eye speaks to Type-A personalities. It has a message for those who need to learn to balance time and responsibilities with leisure or who sacrifice family for work and getting ahead.

Red Tiger Eye teaches us that a quest for perfection may lead to stress, anxiety, and dissatisfaction when the quest becomes more important than relationships and living a balanced life that includes work, but not to the exclusion of play, relaxation, relationships, social occasions, etc.

Red Tiger Eye counsels that while it is noble to strive toward perfection, (actual perfection being unattainable), the striving should not be detrimental to self and others. Red Tiger Eye also tells us that perfection often exists only in our own minds and as such can be unachievable.

In the health readings Red Tiger Eye represents one's need to relax, "let your hair down" once in awhile—to "stop and smell the roses."

The Life Lesson of Red Tiger Eye is, "Embrace imperfection." Look at how perfection exists in Nature. The movement toward perfection is an ongoing process that is never completed in the material realm.

Substitutes: Tiger Iron may substitute for Red Tiger Eye (Tiger Eye/Iron combination stone). Red Garnet, (preferably opaque, such as Almandine Garnet, with many inclusions and striations), or non-gem grade Ruby make good alternates. Staurolite, often called "Fairy Cross" or "Fairy Stone," may be substituted for Red Tiger Eye as well.

RHODOCHROSITE

Rhodocrosite (manganese carbonate, $MnCO_3$) is a gemstone that is rich, rose pink in color due to mineral-manganese, and often has wavy bands of lighter pink to cream and sometimes gray. It is translucent to opaque and forms in medium temperature hydrothermal veins and rarely crystallizes into cubes.

Rhodocrosite is a mineral most often found in sedimentary rock deposits. It is found on the gem market cut into cabochons, tumble polished nodules, or beads.

Rhodocrosite belongs to the "carbonate" family of minerals. In the case of Rhodocrosite, manganese is the predominant metal bonding the triangular ions of carbon and oxygen (CO_3). The triangular nature of the carbon-oxygen ions in Rhodocrosite and other carbonate gemstones (Calcite, Siderite, Dolomite, Smithsonite, Aragonite, Azurite, and Malachite) makes them particularly useful in manifesting and maintaining various conditions based upon their component minerals. The triangular shape of the ions resonates with the ancient mystical Law of the Triangle. Rhodocrosite and other triple carbon-oxygen gemstones have metaphysical potential in bridging the planes of mind, body, and soul—important considerations in the manifestation process where two conditions give rise to a third!

In the readings, Rhodochrosite will attract those who want to forgive but haven't found a way to do so. This gemstone counsels the need to release and let go of trauma, particularly of that associated with love and subsequent betrayal. By releasing resentment we liberate ourselves from enslavement to negative emotions and thoughts. Rhodochrosite attracts those who are on the path of practicing unconditional love and forgiveness, and others who suffer pangs of guilt. This gemstone teaches us to forgive ourselves, as well.

> The Life Lesson of Rhodochrosite is, "Love is all."

In the healing portion of the readings, this stone represents the heart, both in a figurative sense and as a physical organ.

Substitutes: Pink Tourmaline crystals may be substituted for Rhodochrosite in the readings if not substituted elsewhere.

RHODONITE

Rhodonite is a silica-rich gemstone also containing manganese, iron, and magnesium. This gemstone is born of metamorphic processes. Their pink and black colors speak of its messages for humankind. Look for Rhodonite as tumble polished nodules, beads, or cabochons.

The color pink tells us that this mineral reads our heart's desire and its black mottling suggests blessings and other good things arising out of a place of mystery—an abundant Universe whose desire is to fulfill our desires. On an energetic level this gemstone attracts good vibrations. Rhodonite draws the energy of gifts and pleasant surprises!

When selected during a reading Rhodonite's message is that a gift, surprise, or boon is forthcoming. This is usually something unanticipated. This gemstone may also indicate a positive answer (usually with a wonderful surprise attached) to a question asked by a querist. The gift heralded by Rhodonite can be monetary, although not generally. The monetary aspect of the gift brought by Rhodonite, if it is to occur, is usually secondary to some form of news, information, or other type of unexpected good fortune.

The Life Lesson of Rhodonite is, "Expect a miracle."

In a health reading this gemstone represents the lungs and lung tissue.

Substitutes: Rhodonite is easily found and requires no substitute.

ROSE QUARTZ

Rose Quartz is rarely found in Nature as crystals, but generally occurs in non-crystalline masses. It is often cut and lightly faceted along its length to resemble the shape of a natural Quartz Crystal. Its soft pink color is caused by titanium oxide and/or manganese. It is likely that these two component minerals inhibit Rose Quartz from forming into crystal points. The energy of Rose Quartz, therefore, tends to be encircling or embracing rather than directional or bi-directional as with most Quartz Crystals. Rose Quartz suggests gentle nurturing, love and healing, and indeed, this is its message. Rose Quartz may be marketed in the form of small "wands," tumble polished nodules, beads, or cut to resemble Quartz Crystal shapes.

Selecting Rose Quartz during a reading suggests to the querist that healing on some level is needed or will be occurring. Less often this gemstone may indicate that a querist has healing abilities. The stones in the immediate vicinity of Rose Quartz will reveal more information.

Drawn during a health reading, Rose Quartz represents that healing in some area—physical, spiritual, or emotional—is forthcoming.

The Life Lesson of Rose Quartz is, "We are all one."

Substitutes: Rose Quartz is easily found. No substitute should be needed.

SERPENTINE

Serpentine consists mostly of magnesium silicate, sometimes with asbestos. Magnesium "burns away" the detritus of negative emotions from past- and present-life relationships. In color, Serpentine is often a mottled mix of light and dark green, and black and cream. Serpentine usually forms in massive metamorphic deposits often parallel to stringers of gold.

When polished it is opaque and has a waxy luster. Serpentine is said to be the "parent" of gold and chrysotile (a form of asbestos) because stringers of gold and chrysotile are often found sandwiched between deposits. This stone is usually found as rough pieces or tumble polished nodules.

During a reading, Serpentine speaks of longtime or priority relationships in a particular context such as a parent, childhood friend, or best friend—someone known for a time as opposed to someone just met. Serpentine may indicate a spouse of longstanding or an ex-spouse.

Autumn is the time of year indicated by Serpentine should the subject of "time" be important in a particular reading. Rarely, this gemstone may also point to the "autumn" of a relationship through death, divorce, or some other means.

> The Life Lesson of Serpentine is, "The bonds that unite..." Generally, this gemstone has a positive message regarding longtime or blood relationships. However, it also teaches us that we no longer need to incarnate with those who have hurt us in past lives and continue to do so in a present incarnation. Strong emotions—love or hate—bond souls together life after life. Serpentine tells us that we may consciously place the "Guardian of the Threshold" between another soul and our own ending a link that keeps two souls in bondage lifetime after lifetime.

First acknowledge an ongoing negative connection with another soul and release attachment to damaged and negative feelings. Then "decree" that the emotional bond uniting your soul with another be broken perpetually into eternity. Visualize placing the Guardian of the Threshold (however you conceive this concept) between yourself and the one with whom you are severing bonds. The cooperation of the other is not required. The bond has no power if the energy forming it is no longer dual in nature.

Serpentine represents addictions, obsessive behaviors, and compulsions when seen during the health portion of a reading.

Substitutes: Green Nephrite, Green Jade or Jadeite may substitute for Serpentine in the readings.

SNOWFLAKE OBSIDIAN

Snowflake Obsidian is a variety of silica-rich volcanic glass. White flecks in the gemstone are the mineral Cristobalite (silicon dioxide, a silica variant) or "phenocrysts" which are merely large crystals of silica embedded within the structure of the gemstone.

Snowflake Obsidian speaks to us of Yin and Yang, of balance, and being comfortable in one's own body and with one's sexuality and gender. It aids in recognizing harmful patterns and thought forms so that these may be confronted. This is a gemstone commonly found as tumble polished nodules.

In a reading Snowflake Obsidian heralds a union, partnership, or a balance of opposites in some manner. It can speak of getting married, or can indicate partnership in some form.

In other contexts the message of Snowflake Obsidian is one of integration and respect for both female and male energies as they exist within oneself, in others, and in Nature. This stone also speaks of balance and equilibrium. In certain contexts Snowflake Obsidian may aid a querist in pointing out that he or she has a fear or disrespect of the opposite sex or her own sexuality. Look to nearby stones for insight.

The Life Lesson of Snowflake Obsidian is, "Others are the mirror of self."

In the health portion of a reading this stone represents balance. It can also speak to a lack of inner balance due to intolerance and disrespect for others.

Substitutes: Snowflake Obsidian is easily obtained.

SODALITE

Sodalite, born of igneous processes, is most often deep blue in color with white inclusions or striations and contains minerals of aluminum, silica, chlorine, and sodium. Sodalite affirms that wisdom is most often born of experience and the trials of life, the conscious cultivation of integrity, and refinement of one's personal philosophy. Cabochons, small wands, and tumble polished nodules are the usual forms marketed.

The message of Sodalite is one of wisdom and insight. In a reading, Sodalite counsels a querist to avoid decisions based upon habitual or old mental conditioning. This gemstone advises the querist to look inward, listening to one's intuition for new insights.

The Life Lesson of Sodalitet is, "Look within."

In the health portion of a reading Sodalite represents the gall bladder.

Substitutes: Lapis may be substituted for Sodalite in the readings.

SUNSTONE

Sunstone is a type of feldspar and comes in cream, yellow, orange, and red colors. Gem grade Sunstone can be quite costly depending on clarity and color. For the readings it is more cost effective to use a less expensive, more commonly found grade that is usually translucent to opaque with iridescent flashes of red or yellow. Sunstone's warmth of color brings to mind warm, sunny days or the hot, lazy summers of childhood. Its energy is bright and merry. It speaks of the joy of children and playful young animals. Its message to humankind is simply "joy of being." This gemstone helps dissolve the layers of care that keep us from feeling a pure, uncomplicated joy and maintaining a sunny outlook. Look for tumble polished nodules.

Chosen as part of a reading Sunstone counsels one to "lighten up." It advises a querist that moments of joy and delight are on the horizon and to be ready to participate emotionally when they arrive. Sunstone gives a "yes" answer to a question.

Depending upon the surrounding stones chosen by the querist this gemstone may be indicating that the querist is looking for joy missing from his or her life. This is especially the case when more than one Sunstone arises during a reading. Sunstone advises that we be constantly open to the joy that is inherent in life and not shunt it behind the tasks and responsibilities of day-to-day living.

Sunstone also counsels us to find the joy and positive attributes of the life you are living right now and that the grass is not always greener on the other side of the fence! Count your blessings! This stone suggests a respite from our quest for more goods, more money, a better house, a more loving spouse, etc. and appreciate the blessings we are enjoying but may not be acknowledging.

> The Life Lesson of Sunstone is, "There is sunshine in my heart today."
> In the health portion of the readings Sunstone represents the need for sunshine both symbolically and literally. Oddly, this stone also represents the sinuses because bright sunlight can cause one to sneeze!

Substitutes: Yellow Calcite or yellow-dyed White Quartz may be used as a substitute for Sunstone.

TIGER EYE

Tiger Eye is a form of crystalline quartz that contains fibers of asbestos (hydrous magnesium silicate). It is born of metamorphic processes and therefore can alter negative energy into something with a positive outcome. In its golden coloration, Tiger Eye was once commonly used to protect its wearer from curses and ill wishing. Wands, small spheres, and tumble polished nodules are the most common forms on the market.

In a reading Tiger Eye points to success, positive results, and good outcomes in spite of any appearances to the contrary. Tiger Eye may attract those who tend to be loners in much the same way as the jungle cat, Tiger, for which this stone is named. Tiger Eye tends to attract those who value their personal freedom often choosing to remain single or even celibate. This gemstone indicates a "yes" answer to a question.

The Life Lesson of Tiger Eye is, "There is light at the end of the tunnel!"

In the health portion of a reading Tiger Eye represents the eyes, vision, the way we see ourselves, and self-esteem.

Substitutions: Tiger Eye is easily found and doesn't require substitution.

TURQUOISE

Turquoise (hydrated copper aluminum phosphate) has long been used as a stone to bring peace, contentment, healing, and protection. It was once believed to alter its color if danger or poison threatened its wearer. Turquoise most often forms in arid regions as an alteration (or secondary) mineral of aluminum-bearing rocks.

Metaphysically this means that Turquoise has evolved or "refined" its vibratory quality. This gemstone's metaphysical mission is to bring vibrations of peace to the planet and humankind!

In a gemstone reading, Turquoise assures a querist that peace, satisfaction, and contentment are the natural birthrights of humankind. When appearing as an answer to a question, Turquoise answers in the affirmative. Turquoise promises a return to peace after a time of turbulence.

THE HIDDEN MESSAGES WITHIN CRYSTALS AND GEMSTONES

The Life Lesson of Turquoise is, "Peace profound."

Turquoise represents the ears, ability to hear, and listen when selected during the health portion of a reading.

Substitutes: Turquoise is easily found but has become very expensive. Magnesite that has been dyed or colored blue (called "Turqurenite" or "Turquoisite") is an acceptable and affordable option.

Neither Turquoise nor Magnesite are silicates, and while chemically different, do carry on one level of their vibratory expression a similar mineral message. In addition, blue-dyed Magnesite and Turquoise are similar in texture and physical appearance. Use either in the divination collection.

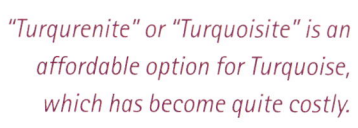

"Turqurenite" or "Turquoisite" is an affordable option for Turquoise, which has become quite costly.

TURRITELLA AGATE

This stone is sometimes called "Fossil Agate" and is identified as a dark brown, almost black agate containing the fossilized shells of tiny sea snails. The silica shell-replacements are usually white or cream in color.

While actual shell material no longer remains, the shell form has been preserved by silica precipitate.

Along seacoasts worldwide ancient people looked to the sea as a source of food and a byway upon which to travel. Beautiful shells from coastal areas were used for adornment and traded with inland dwellers for needed commodities. Shells once had monetary value and were used as a form of currency. The fossilized shells of Turritella Agate add another aspect to this gemstone because they contain the vibrations of abundance. Our ancestors rightly intuited this when they used beautiful shells of all types to represent the concept of material wealth. This gemstone is most often marketed as tumble polished nodules.

Turritella Agate has a message to relate regarding money. This gemstone usually advises an increase in monetary wealth, usually based upon merit, talent, or a job well done. This may take the form of a raise in pay, a cash advance, or bonus. Merit, rather than an unearned monetary gift, is usually attached to money indicated by Turritella Agate. If more than one Turritella Agate is drawn during a reading, this means "a greater amount" is likely to be coming "sooner." Depending upon surrounding stones, more than one may also indicate a need for money rather than its increase.

The Life Lesson of Turritella Agate is, "Life goes on in one form or another."

In the health portion of a reading, this Agate represents the kidneys, bladder, and urinary tract.

Substitutes: If for some reason, Turritella Agate is unavailable when you assemble your divination collection, Green Aventurine (if not already used as a substitute), or tumble polished nodules of Mother-of-pearl, Abalone, or Cowry shells may be used.

UNAKITE

Unakite contains feldspar, silica, and epidote. Feldspar aids in shedding old habits and limitations, silica retains and transmits information, and epidote (hydrous calcium aluminum iron silicate) is a metamorphic mineral whose composition has been altered due to various Earth processes thereby aiding and abetting change.

THE HIDDEN MESSAGES WITHIN CRYSTALS AND GEMSTONES

Unakite presents a pale- to medium-green and red color combination. Wands, beads, cabochons, and tumble polished nodules are the most commonly found forms on the market.

In a gemstone reading Unakite brings a warning that stress, anxiety, and tension, if left untended may result—or has already resulted—in physical pain and illness. This gemstone advises the querist to look at his or her life and identify those issues that may be causing stress and pain. It may be finance, romance, work, or family-related. Selection of Unakite reveals that the querist may be mismanaging his or her energy by "burning the candle at both ends." A more sinister connotation of this gemstone is that of "living a double life" as in a "Dr. Jekyll and Mr. Hyde" context. In this case there is usually misconduct or misrepresentation regarding one or more aspects of life.

The Life Lesson of Unakite is, "Identify what is pushing your buttons."

In the health reading, Unakite represents the need to prioritize and to get to root causes of stress. One cause of stress is a tendency to rate every chore, responsibility, and obligation with equal value.

Substitutes: Pale-green Jasper or Agate may substitute for Unakite.

YELLOW QUARTZ

Yellow Quartz is a translucent silicate of igneous origin. Yellow Quartz has a warm, luminous energy. It has the ability to allow us to feel comfortable in our environment, whether that is a "place" or our own bodies. Yellow Quartz calls us home to our "ground of being" and helps us feel "at home" in our surroundings. Thus it speaks to us of "home" or "hearth fires."

Home, for some, may mean the land of one's ancestors, the country of one's origin, or an adopted new place. Home may be a cozy, country cottage or a sleek New York-style loft.

Look for tumble polished nodules as the most commonly sold forms.

The concept of "hearth" most often signifies the structure we call "home." Querists who draw Yellow Quartz have an affinity for some aspect of home management, such as "home arts." Thus people who are interested in interior decorating, designing, building, or "keeping house," or a "homebody" would likely be attracted to this gemstone.

What does the word "home" evoke? For some it is a charming country cottage.

THE HIDDEN MESSAGES WITHIN CRYSTALS AND GEMSTONES

> The Life Lesson of Yellow Quartz is, "Bloom where you are planted." Because this gemstone represents the concept of "home," it counsels us to feel "at home" in our bodies and to nourish both body and the home environment by creating a serene, pleasant space—to gently, creatively, and thoughtfully feather our own nest!

Substitutes: Yellow Onyx, Honey Onyx, or Yellow Jasper may be substituted.

• • • • • • •

You have now met the crystals and gemstones—and a pair of gemstone fraternal twins—which comprise the divination collection and learned their significant, primary mineral messages. Knowing the primary messages of each type of crystal and gemstone in the divination set brings you into resonance with its frequency and vibration, thus opening the door to further inter-realm communication.

Knowing the Life Lesson of each opens one to a wealth of mineral wisdom that act as signposts along the way to personal growth. The health portion of any reading gives valuable insights into achieving and maintaining health and balance.

The next chapter comprises a subsequent step on our shared journey—that of learning the techniques used when giving crystal and gemstone readings.

CHAPTER 3

••••••••••

What Is Crystal and Gemstone Divination?

Throughout history and among various cultures worldwide there have been many systems for "casting the stones" to foretell future events and to receive guidance. The system outlined in these pages is a compilation of several of those plus my own experiences with crystals and gemstones.

Over the last three decades I have refined the system revealed to me by the stones themselves, a system initially received in meditation and subsequently used to give myself and others readings.

This simple-to-learn, very effective method of divination uses thirty-eight different types of colorful crystals and gemstones that were introduced in the previous chapter. A set of forecasting stones includes three of each variety for a total of one hundred fourteen stones.

Each stone in the set should be approximately three-quarter to one-inch in diameter for ease in seeing and handling for both yourself and those to whom you give

Author's original 30-year-old divination set.

readings. Quartz Crystals are best when less than two inches in length. However, these size suggestions are only guidelines. It is more important to have the energy of the stones or their substitutes than to adhere strictly to size guidelines. The only cautions are having your stones neither too small nor too large. Select what is available and comfortable to work with.

An entire collection of divination stones takes up little space and is easily transportable. If you locate stones that are a bit bigger or smaller than the recommended size, go ahead and get them. It is better to have the right stones than be too concerned about their size as long as they are not too small to easily identify—or pick up—or so big that they overwhelm the rest of the collection.

Gemstones from my original divination set are harmonious in color, size, and shape.

A set of forecasting stones is beautiful and useful. The energies of the collected stones are extraordinary and may be used to positively energize any space where they are placed. A special dish, basket, or tray displays the stones in an aesthetic manner and is both a container and an aid for selection and reading the stones. A black fabric lining sewn or glued into a basket or tray makes each stone easy to see and cushions them from chipping or cracking when stirred and moved about during the selection process of a reading.

For my stones I use a round flat basket—the type used to hold paper plates at picnics and barbecues—into which I stitched black velvet. This has served my divination crystal and gemstone set for over two decades. This tray also serves my new set of divination stones.

WHAT IS CRYSTAL AND GEMSTONE DIVINATION? 65

In addition to my old set of stones, I have compiled a new collection of crystals and gemstones that reflect what is available and reasonably priced on the mineral market today. The old and new sets vary only in the addition or deletion of a few hard-to-find or costly gemstones.

A tray ten to twelve inches in diameter is usually large enough so that all the stones comprise a single colorful, sparkling layer. Having each stone equally visible makes for the best forecasting results. If your stones lie upon one another, selection becomes difficult and the reading's results may seem clouded or inconclusive. When traveling I carry my divination stones safely and securely in a fabric pouch.

In this type of crystal and gemstone reading the stones are not actually "cast" or "thrown." Instead they are selected one at a time and set down on a pad or scarf.

Stones are not "cast" but instead are selected and placed upon a pad or scarf.

The Basics of Reading the Stones

To perform an overall or general reading the querist is asked to select nine stones from the tray one at a time and lay each on a piece of fabric, a scarf, or pad. This scarf or pad should be used only for your crystal and gemstone forecasting. I made a simple, attractive, and functional pad from a magazine over which I stitched a piece of black velvet. Black or dark blue fabric shows the gemstones to their best advantage.

Nine stones are usually all that needs to be selected during the first phase of the reading. The first nine set the tone of the reading and become the basis for seeking further information. After the stones have been selected and laid on the pad the reader notes their meaning and proximity to one another.

To begin the reading the querist selects nine stones and lays them on the pad.

This initial nine-stone layout is for bringing to the forefront issues presently and soon to be affecting the querist. Issues addressed in this phase are usually those concerned with relationships, career, home, recreation, and prosperity, but not limited to just these subjects. After revealing to the querist the messages of the first nine stones, the reader removes them from the pad and returns them to the tray. At this point I ask the querist if she has any questions regarding the reading, thus far. If so, the querist is directed to select three more stones while holding in mind the question she wishes to ask.

After the stones are laid down I interpret their messages for the querist. She may seek further clarification if needed by selecting three more stones. If the querist is satisfied with the answer she may select three stones to answer any other questions on remaining issues of concern. Using the three-stone question-and-answer process the querist may ask questions regarding the

WHAT IS CRYSTAL AND GEMSTONE DIVINATION? 67

nine-stone layout or any issues of concern that haven't been addressed yet. After each question has been answered the stones are always returned to the tray prior to the next question. When the gemstones relay information about future events these may not always make sense to the querist until the passage of time brings them into her experience.

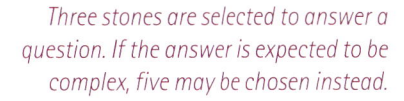

Three stones are selected to answer a question. If the answer is expected to be complex, five may be chosen instead.

A health reading is generally the last layout of a divination session and comprises a selection of five stones. I always ask if the querist desires a health reading. Not all do.

Five stones may be chosen for the health portion of a reading.

As seen in the previous chapter each crystal and gemstone not only has its primary message and Life Lesson, but also bears an affinity to a certain part of the human (or animal) body that becomes significant during the health portion of any reading. Additional stones may be selected to answer questions if health issues emerge that require more information or clarification. Health questions are answered using the same three-stone selection process used in the previous phases of the reading.

When you give readings on a regular basis to a querist, he or she becomes a valued client. On a subsequent visit a querist is very likely to tell you how information revealed by a previous reading that made little sense at the time did, in fact, come true. She or he may relate specifics of how this occurred and marvel at how an event came to pass "just as predicted in the reading!"

How the Gemstone Selection Process Works

When giving a reading I ask the querist to pick nine stones that "draw," "speak," or "call out" in some way. The querist may assume she is attracted to particular stones by color or luster. Sometimes stones are chosen because they engender a particular feeling in the querist. Often a querist will mention that a certain stone or stones "drew" her attention but will have difficulty describing why. She may say, "This stone just attracted me for some reason." Stones selected will vary from reading to reading for each querist.

Crystals and gemstones that have something to impart "invite" or "demand" the querist's attention. Other stones not needed seem to "withdraw," going "unseen," or unnoticed by the querist.

The querist's selection of stones will vary with each reading given over a period of weeks, months, or years. In my experience no querist has ever selected the same groups of stones from one reading to the next despite the fact that she may favor certain ones for wearing or healing.

I have heard time and again, "My favorite stone is amethyst (for example) but for some reason I am drawn to pick up Tiger Eye (etc.) instead." The querist *will* pick the crystals and gemstones right for the reading she is receiving at any particular time.

The querist, in most cases, will not know the divinatory messages of the crystals and gemstones even if he or she performs metaphysical work with stones on a regular basis. *The divinatory messages of the stones may be related to but are not always the same as their metaphysical or spiritual definitions.*

WHAT IS CRYSTAL AND GEMSTONE DIVINATION?

If you happen to be giving a reading to a querist well-practiced in the methods of crystal and gemstone divination revealed by this book, merely have the querist close his or her eyes before selecting any of the stones. The querist will be drawn through touch and vibrational attraction to the stones he or she needs. While such a querist would certainly be able to do a reading for himself or herself, sometimes it is helpful to receive a reading through the lens of someone else's perspective and insight into gemstone wisdom. Sometimes we are just too close to our own issues to see them from an unbiased perspective.

On occasion I've had a querist select nine stones during the initial phase of the reading only to state emphatically that another is strongly attracting her and she simply must select that one also. If this occurs allow the querist to make a tenth selection, but not too many more than that. Wanting to select a number of additional stones may indicate a high degree of indecisiveness in the querist regarding choices and situations.

Indecision regarding the selection of a stone may hint that the querist is unsure which course to follow regarding an issue. Dropping a stone may indicate a direction or issue that should be pursued but was abandoned due to lack of information. Perhaps the querist has misgivings as to the outcome if one path is chosen over another. Crystal and gemstone wisdom will help the querist choose the answer she needs. I recently gave a reading in which the querist selected her initial nine stones but then after laying them down proceeded to rearrange them into different patterns for several minutes. I read the stones as they lay there and as soon as I was finished she rearranged them again! I felt this was significant and recorded the new arrangement, as well. A fresh slant on the previous arrangement produced a message of significance to the querist and issues she was confronting at the time. It turned out that this querist was deeply engaged in rearranging various aspects of her life such as health, community involvement, and relationships, as well as her spiritual and inner life. The readings and how they unfold will reveal amazing aspects to both reader and querist.

> Take note if a querist selects a stone and accidentally drops it, seems unsure about a selection, or replaces a stone in the basket and chooses another. These seemingly random processes are not accidental. They are important and telling clues significant to the overall issues affecting the querist.

Stones appearing in a closely related group may reveal related aspects of a message or layers of information on a topic. A stone apart from the main group or on the edge of the scarf or mat may indicate that the issue it addresses is of less importance, or perhaps that issue will not manifest until time has passed. Crystals and gemstones placed to the top or center of the scarf or pad generally address issues of greatest importance.

Depending upon the proximity of the stones and their placement individually or in a related group, you (the reader) might feel prompted by the gemstones to present either their primary message, a variation the gemstones intuit to you, or simply the Life Lesson inherent to each stone. A stone's Life Lesson—its wisdom in a nutshell—is often the very answer sought by the querist.

Should a querist select two or even all three, of a particular variety of gemstone additional importance or weight is given to that issue. This may indicate a strong need in the life of the querist. It may indicate that the issue is in the near future, as well.

> As reader, your role is to relate to the querist the messages the stones have for him or her. The primary communication between the human and mineral realms takes place between stones and reader on behalf of the querist. The reader merely acts as the intermediary between the querist and the messages the stones wish to convey.

When I first began reading crystals and gemstones for others, the less I knew about the life and questions the querist brought to a reading the better and more accurate the reading turned out to be. If I knew something about an issue it could interfere with the subtle whisperings of the mineral realm. Time and working with the crystals and gemstones resolved this problem for me. I simply learned to switch off what I knew and listen for subtle whisperings from the mineral realm instead.

With practice, a reader begins to absorb information from the stones that transcends their primary messages and Life Lessons. The stones begin to "speak" in greater detail revealing surprising information that will astound both querist and reader alike! The manner in which the stones speak is varied. You may "hear" words arising in your mind. You may have a strong urge to voice something to a querist related to the gemstone in question. Or, you may simply have a feeling, hunch, or intuition.

Before you begin giving readings to others, the best form of practice is to give them to yourself. In this situation you will be both querist and reader. The only difference is that you will select stones with your eyes closed.

Select each stone and lay it on the pad. Just be sure you know where the basket and pad are before you close your eyes! I find that closing my eyes is necessary because I know the meaning of the stones and I might subconsciously select stones that would altar the reading in a false or negative manner. Be assured you will select, albeit blindly, the stones you need to answer your questions and concerns.

Crystal and gemstone readings are a "stand alone" system but may be used alongside other systems of divination. Several stones in a divination set have meanings similar to Tarot cards, for example. These particular stones and the Tarot cards they echo will be identified in Chapter 6—*Gemstone Forecasting and Other Divination Systems*. It has been my experience that on the occasions I have given a reading to myself or others using both gemstones and Tarot cards the readings are complimentary, reiterating analogous messages sometimes from different but congruous perspectives.

Keeping Records

Most querists want a chronicle of their readings so they can refer to it as time and events transpire. There are several ways to record the reading. I will share my rather low-tech method that I've become comfortable with over time. Feel free to create one that works best for you.

While giving a reading I usually make a quick drawing of the position of each crystal and gemstone selected by the querist, including three-stone answers to questions. Next to each image I've drawn, I quickly pencil the name of the gemstone. My drawings aren't fancy. I just make a quick sketch of the approximate location of each crystal and gemstone on the pad and its proximity to the others. I use this sketch as a reference when compiling the results of the reading. In the past I used to mail a typewritten chronicle and sketch of the reading to the querist within a few days.

In the 1980s and early '90s I simply made my quick illustrations and tape-recorded the reading while it was being given. The taped cassette and copy of the sketch were sent home with the querist.

These days a reading may be emailed or even videotaped. Instead of a rough sketch and taped reading being sent home with a querist I use my computer's "draw" program to create a stylish schematic of the reading. This and a nicely typed chronicle of the reading are then e-mailed to the querist. See the Crystal Index on the next three pages.

Keep a record of your self-readings too. For this purpose an inexpensive journal works well or you can record them on your computer. Be sure to back up your self-readings to disk or CD in case your computer crashes.

Ethics of Giving a Crystal and Gemstone Reading

When doing a divination for a querist I never ask why the querist has come. Often issues of a personal or private nature are the basis for someone wanting a reading. I relate only what the stones have indicated and ask if it makes sense to the querist. This puts the querist at ease regarding personal topics. Usually toward the end of a reading a querist opens up somewhat and relates how some point, or points, brought forth by the reading has helped to solve a problem or bring greater insight.

A tendency to insert one's own advice can arise when the reader knows something of the life and issues facing a querist. This can result in the reader giving what he or she thinks the stones are saying rather than tuning into what they are actually trying to convey. It is important to completely remove personal ego and what one "thinks is best" for the querist and instead tune into what the stones are transmitting.

With practice a reader learns to shut off information or preconceived ideas that may affect a reading. Another thing to watch for is when a querist requests a reading that reveals issues upon which the reader has a moral or religious bias. If this happens it is vitally important to the ethics of the reading to tune into what the stones are communicating and leave personal views out of the equation.

Religious and moral views can vary between individuals, cultures, and religions. At best humans have an imperfect understanding of God's laws. While we like to remain convinced that our own beliefs are immutable in their correctness, try to leave personal biases or "truths" out of consideration during a reading.

The greater world of Spirit is in a better position to judge these things then we mere mortals. Let Divine Intelligence reign on issues of judgment. Remember that the mineral realm has a perspective covering vast epochs of time long before and after our species arose. Trust mineral wisdom to provide the correct answers and perspectives on issues.

WHAT IS CRYSTAL AND GEMSTONE DIVINATION? 73

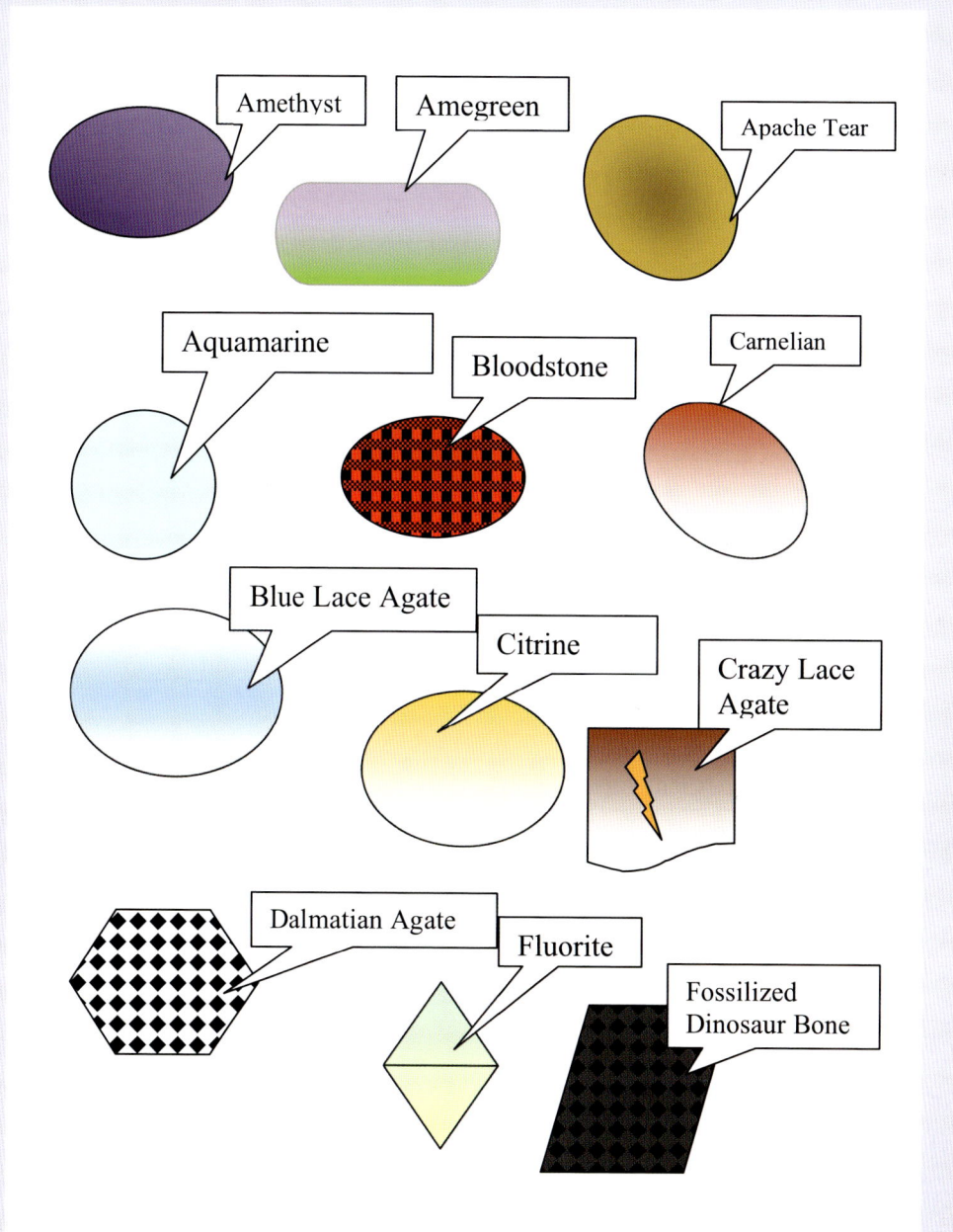

- Amethyst
- Amegreen
- Apache Tear
- Aquamarine
- Bloodstone
- Carnelian
- Blue Lace Agate
- Citrine
- Crazy Lace Agate
- Dalmatian Agate
- Fluorite
- Fossilized Dinosaur Bone

Crystal Index

74 CRYSTAL AND GEMSTONE DIVINATION

Girasol

Labradorite

Hematite

Lepidolite

Lined Agate

Magnesite

Malachite

Moonstone

Moss Agate

Pink Aventurine

Pyrite

Quartz Crystal

Red Tiger Eye

Red Jasper

Crystal Index

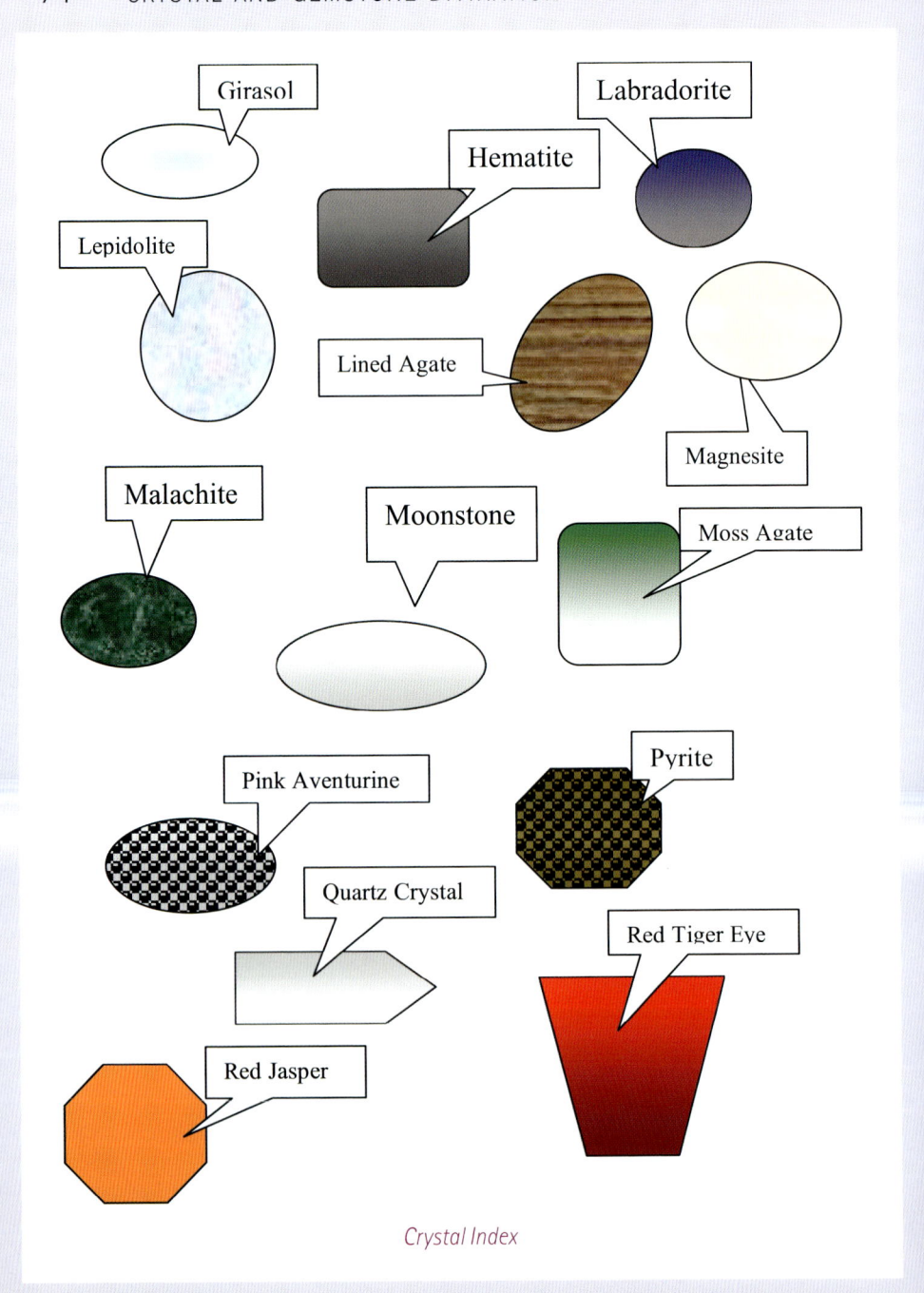

WHAT IS CRYSTAL AND GEMSTONE DIVINATION? 75

Rhodocrosite

Rhodonite

Rose Quartz

Snowflake Obsidian

Serpentine

Sunstone

Sodalite

Turquoise

Tiger Eye

Yellow Quartz

Turritella Agate

Unakite

Crystal Index

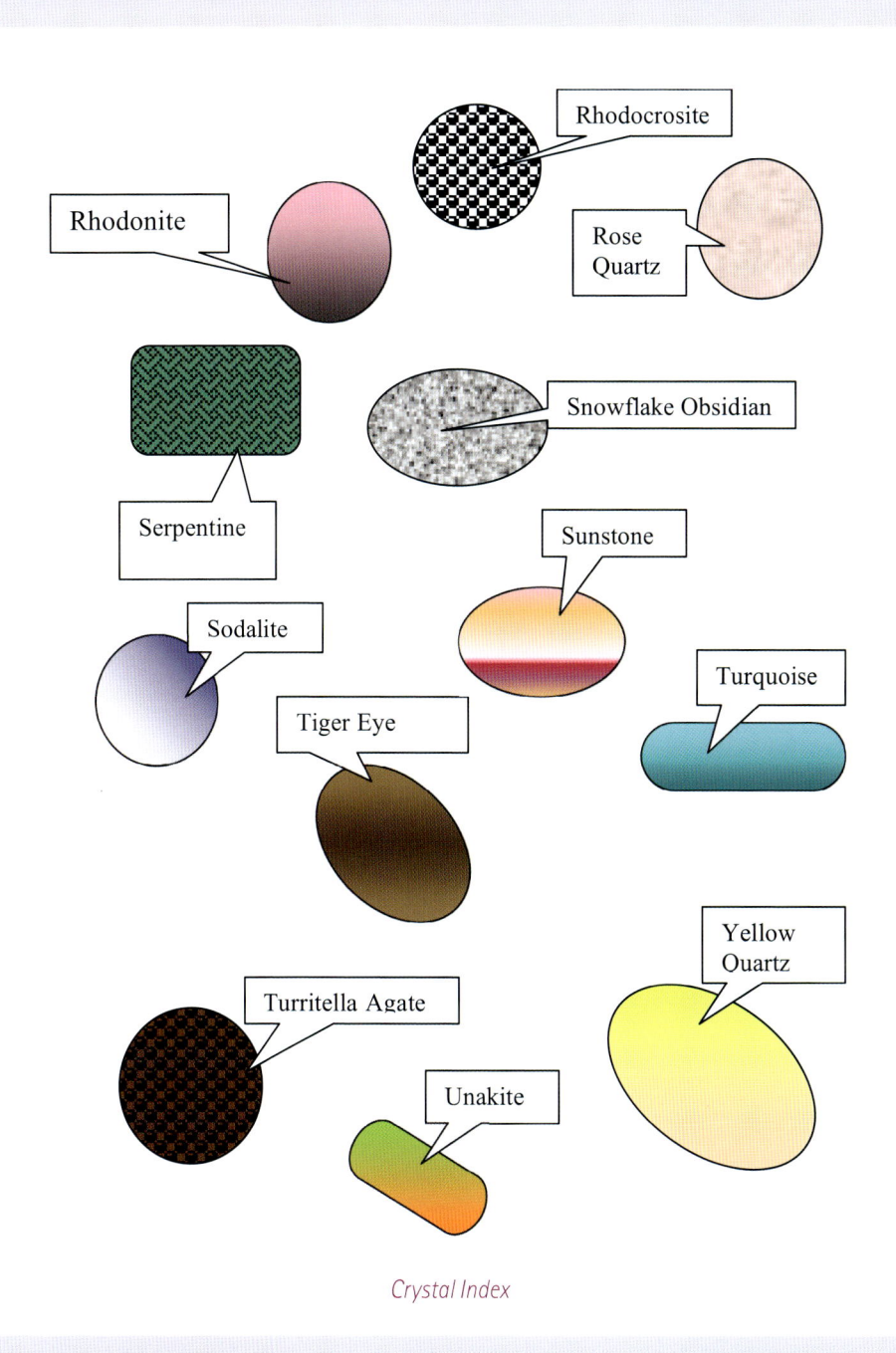

If a querist should reveal something during a reading that is criminal in nature or a behavior or plan that would create physical harm to another, then the reader is ethics-bound to inform the authorities.

For example, if someone should confess to murder, or child endangering, or a proposed bank heist—something of a criminal nature that would harm others or place them as risk—then the reader should inform the authorities that a crime has or will likely take place.

I am often asked if it is ethical to charge money for a reading. In our culture there is a saying that, "time is money." Time, your time and mine, has a monetary value and you should feel at ease charging for time given for a reading. Money is a form of energy. You are giving your energy, via the reading, and the querist is contributing energy in a tangible form…money.

> From an ethical standpoint a reader should never gossip about the personal content of a querist's reading.

Barter is another tangible form of return. The querist may bring something of value needed by the reader. In a rural area this might consist of garden produce, eggs, or a handmade item for which the querist is well known.

Services are another form of exchange. A reading may be exchanged for a service the querist can provide such as an automobile tune-up, home organization, or baby-sitting (if the reader and querist are well known to one another). The options for exchange of energy are endless. Generally, however, money is the type of energy most provided by the querist, at least in the initial stages of the relationship.

Crystal and gemstone divination is an art whose horizons are continually expanding and deepening. After almost thirty years (how time flies!) of giving crystal and gemstone readings I am still on a wondrous journey of discovery! It is my joy and delight—and blessing—to share the mystical gift of communion available and awaiting you in the mineral realms. Reading this book and applying the techniques is only the first step on a wondrous, lifelong journey.

CHAPTER 4

• • • • • • • • • • •

The Self-Reading and Gemstone Interpretation

As MENTIONED IN THE PREVIOUS CHAPTER, one of the best methods for learning how to use your crystal and gemstone collection for divination is by giving readings to yourself. I like to do a self-reading about once a week so I know what to be on the lookout for that may be entering my experience.

Self-readings are a wonderful method for working with each stone's primary message, Life Lesson, and what part of the body-mind-spirit it represents. Because I usually give myself a reading once a week I don't always include the health portion unless I need to address a specific health issue. A health reading three or four time a year for me is usually enough.

Self-readings aid in developing a strong relationship with your crystals and gemstones, promote intercommunication, and keep those channels open and functioning. Self-readings are wonderful practice for interpreting multi-faceted messages inherent when stones occur in the layout as groups.

Frequently crystals or gemstones appear that have nothing to do with the issue or concern for which you're conducting your self-reading. These may be warning of impending trouble, conflict, or problems entering your sphere of influence. Likewise, unforeseen positive change or good news could be heading your way.

> Crystals and gemstones may not always tell you what you want to hear. Instead, you may be told what you need to hear!

Record Keeping for Learning and Self-Transformation

A record of your self-readings becomes a wonderful tool for tracking your crystal and gemstone readings and interpretations. Being able to look at how you interpreted a reading in comparison to how events unfolded is invaluable for refining your interpretative skills.

Used as a tool for self-transformation, a record of my readings is helpful for tracking the manner in which trends and cycles have unfolded over the years. I can observe, with hindsight, those times when I followed gemstone wisdom and succeeded. And, I am reminded of times when I stubbornly violated my own better judgment (and the advice of the crystals and gemstones) and sabotaged my own outcomes. I've discovered recurring tendencies to make the same mistakes in regards to relationships, destructive habits, and finances. If you record your self-readings you will see if any trends and issues tend to repeat in cycles throughout your life.

These are just some of the journals I have filled with self-readings over the years.

Over the years I've filled several journals with self-readings. Each reading is recorded on a fresh page, or pages. For each I record the date and jot down at the top of the page a simple sentence briefly outlining the issue for that day's reading. However, because I give myself a reading once a week there is not always a specific issue to be addressed. In that case I simply write, "General Reading" next to the date. If there is an issue I want to address, I jot down a few words that represent my issue, such as, "My vacation next month," or "About the guy I just met," and so on.

Below the date and subject of the self-reading I sketch each stone and its position in relation to others in the layout. Next to each stone's sketch I pencil in its name. Below my illustration I'll pen my impressions, interpretations, and any intuitions received from the mineral realm during the reading.

As issues addressed in a reading begin to unfold I record those outcomes in the journal also. While a reading may address an issue that will manifest at a future time, the precise details and who is involved may not be known until the event occurs. It's interesting to see how predicted energies and issues evolve into actual events.

Based upon my self-readings I've developed a great deal of faith in the efficacy of mineral wisdom and come to rely on weekly forecasts. Regardless of how you choose to chronicle your self-readings, I'm sure you will find doing so an invaluable aid.

Interpretation of Gemstone Messages

I'd like to share some of my self-readings with you to illustrate how gemstones reveal their messages in the context of a reading. Instead of reproducing my pencil sketches which might be confusing and make things more difficult to understand, I have included photo illustrations of the self-readings. Seeing both the illustrations and the interpretations will be more helpful than just reading descriptions alone. These examples of my self-readings will help to illustrate how stones in close proximity—as a related group—reveal layers of information regarding issues. You will also see how the stones in a layout reveal information and how I have interpreted it. For these examples of self-readings, I will keep to the primary messages of each stone as given in Chapter 2, The Hidden Messages of Crystals and Gemstones. In time the mineral realm will begin to reveal to you additional messages beyond the primary messages.

To give myself a reading I select—with eyes closed—each stone and lay it down on the pad, until nine have been chosen. I keep my eyes shut until all nine stones have been selected and set down. I don't try to identify the stones as I touch them, or think about laying them down in any particular fashion. I just aim for the pad and let things unfold as they will. If a particular issue is being addressed I hold that thought in mind as I select the stones.

Choosing stones with closed eyes may feel haphazard but the right stones and their layout on the pad always occurs in the right manner for any issue being addressed. This is mineral wisdom at work!

After opening my eyes, I take a few moments to observe any patterns or groupings of stones on the pad. A quick sketch of the position of each stone and its name is noted in my journal. For me sketching the position of each stone and jotting down its name seems to enhance the opening of the channel to the mineral realm.

Domination by conscious awareness, I believe, prevents us from receiving subtle impressions arising from our inner wisdom and deeper knowing. Inner wisdom and deep knowing is the space, void, or gap between our everyday thoughts where we can connect with other realms. I, like most people, have a hard time turning off my conscious mind so that I can make this connection.

> When I first started working with divination stones, the harder I tried to receive information beyond the primary gemstone messages, the less I got. In our culture the conscious mind tends to dominate our waking hours, only relinquishing its grasp during sleep or deep meditation.

While my conscious mind is engaged in its task of drawing and jotting names it cannot throw up its continual barrage of thoughts—one after another in a continual procession! This leaves my subconscious free to receive and transmit impressions without interference. By giving the conscious mind a simple task to keep it occupied and out of the way my subconscious/psychic awareness is able to slip through with communications from the mineral realm. Perhaps this simple technique will work for you too!

I know well, after many years, the basic message of each stone in my divination set so if additional information arises I jot it down. If no intuitive information is forthcoming it means I merely need to record a stone's basic message for that reading.

THE SELF-READING AND GEMSTONE INTERPRETATION

To read stones appearing as a related group, the primary message (or intuitive message, if received) is considered as well as how their combined messages give variety and depth of meaning to an issue. By interpreting the combined messages of a group of stones it is possible to glean multi-faceted details regarding a subject.

Before we look at my self-readings, let's consider a few simple examples consisting of only two or three stones so you get an idea of how to interpret the *individual* messages of a *group* of stones to get a more complex meaning.

Say, for instance that as part of a nine-stone layout you see that certain gemstones lie in close proximity forming a group. Let's imagine that **Turritella Agate** and **Fossilized Dinosaur Bone** are quite close together.

Turritella Agate—with a primary message of an increase in money through merit—is in close proximity to **Fossilized Dinosaur Bone**—change in work or professional status. It would be likely that this combination has a message concerning a raise in pay due to promotion or advancement.

In a related example, you observe that **Crazy Lace Agate**—relocation, movement, or home change—appears in close proximity to **Turritella Agate** and **Fossilized Dinosaur Bone**. A likely interpretation would be, "My current employer will transfer me to another locale which will result in a raise in pay."

Let's swap **Crazy Lace Agate** for **Citrine** in your three-stone group. Now we have **Turritella Agate, Fossilized Dinosaur Bone**, and **Citrine**—new beginning or change. A likely message these three stones are conveying is, "Employment with a new company will result in my receiving a raise in pay."

Do you see how each gemstone in a group can add a layer of meaning to give you more information regarding an issue?

Here's another example. Let's say that **Amethyst**—spiritual matters—appears in your self-reading. By itself, this gemstone may be advising the need for integrating a spiritual aspect into your life in some form. Stones in close proximity will add additional layers of information.

If **Amethyst** is combined with **Aquamarine**—teacher, rational thought, left-brain thinking—a likely message may be to seek the counsels of a spiritual teacher or adviser to gain insight into some issue in your life. This combination may also be addressing your desire to be a spiritual counselor (if that is the case), or perhaps the combination refers to your profession as a spiritual teacher, priest, or counselor. Depending upon your life situation you could interpret this combination a number of ways.

What if in my self-reading I drew **Amethyst** and **Red Tiger Eye**—zealotry, ego, perfectionism, intolerance, ultra-high standards for self and others—and they lay in close proximity to one another? I may interpret this combination to mean, "I need to be vigilant against intolerance regarding the spiritual beliefs of others," or, that "my ego is interfering with my own spiritual development." Perhaps these two stones are cautioning me regarding a tendency to neglect important facets of my life in favor of pursuing spiritual attainment.

An **Amethyst** paired with **Fluorite**—skill, craft, expertise in practical application—could be advising me to think about writing (because that is my craft) a book or article on a spiritual subject. If I had no subject in mind then I would consider being open to an idea that would soon be presented in some way. Sometimes stones appear in a reading to alert us to be on the lookout for a "sign," "omen," or opportunity.

You may be asking how to decide which interpretation is the correct one when several potentials exist. This is where mineral wisdom will guide you—this and practice working with the stones. There is nothing wrong with jotting down several possible interpretations then biding your time and seeing which manifests. This is part of the learning process. When doing self-readings you will know a good deal of the time which interpretation best fits your particular life experience.

When doing a reading for another you may not always know which interpretation fits. When this occurs I relate all the potentials letting the querist decide which interpretation best fits his or her circumstance. It is likely you won't always know or get a feeling which interpretation is the precise one. Sometimes more than one potential exists because outcomes are based upon decisions we will make that determine the actual outcome.

Wisdom comes through learning how to make choices for ourselves. The crystals and gemstones will direct our attention to an issue and its various potentials. Some will be positive and some negative. Which path we actually choose remains our own choice, be it right or wrong. A self-reading may advise that an action will have negative outcomes. Yet, for one reason or another, we choose to take the negative route. This is how we learn.

> We always have free will. Our future exists as a series of "potentials." Through our free will to make choices we can create an outcome from several potentials.

THE SELF-READING AND GEMSTONE INTERPRETATION 83

Mineral wisdom gives querists that same opportunity when we read for others. More on giving readings to others will be covered in the next chapter.

Let's look at another imaginary group of stones. Let's say I'm considering going into business with an acquaintance. We've drawn up our business plan and are preparing to get a loan to help with setup costs and I decide to do a self-reading regarding these issues. In my reading, three gemstones form a group. **Malachite**—speaks of a need for protection and being on guard, **Dalmatian Agate**—legal issues and contracts, and **Pyrite** —betrayal, deception, the need to investigate.

The other six stones in the reading address the business's issues in a positive manner and indicate a successful outcome. Based upon the results of this reading I see that the business in general will be a positive experience. However, some legal or contractual aspect is in question.

Checking our business agreement and procedural plan doesn't show any cause for concern. Next I read the fine print of our proposed business loan and see potential problems. I see that while the initial interest rate is reasonable, it is variable in nature, late payment penalties are excessive, and that other terms of the loan are equally dubious.

As a result of this reading I consult my partner and we canvas other lending institutions. We apply for a loan elsewhere with better interest rates and more benevolent terms.

Following are some examples of self-readings from my files. These examples will help to illustrate how crystals and gemstones may be read to relate future events.

SELF-READING #1

The illustration on the next page is of a self-reading conducted on July 4, 2004. Look first at the illustration to see the positions of the stones, and then note how the layout was interpreted.

The reason for the reading in this illustration was my concern regarding a publication for which I'd been writing for several years. I was feeling restless and dissatisfied due to a personality conflict with the editor. The conflict had begun a couple of years prior and seemed to be getting worse. I needed direction and hoped a gemstone reading would guide me toward a positive means of once and for all resolving the problem.

As I held these issues in mind, I closed my eyes and selected each stone and laid it on the mat until nine had been chosen. The following six stones appeared in close proximity to one another and I read them as a group.

Lined Agate—conflict and disturbance.
Fluorite—craft, expertise, or skill in practical application.
Lepidolite—tradition, habit, knowing when to let go.
Moss Agate—love of Nature, outdoors, green and growing things.
Rhodonite—heart's desire and a boon or gift.
Magnesite—karma or grace.

I interpreted this upper grouping as follows: **Lined Agate** spoke of conflict and disturbance surrounding the relationship with the editor of one of the publications for which I was writing. **Magnesite** in close proximity indicated to me that a karmic condition was in play over which I had little control. **Lepidolite** advised me that it was time to let go of the relationship with that publication.

Fluorite spoke of the practical application of my writing skill. Moss Agate directed my attention toward green and growing things—my garden! Rhodonite advised me of a gift or boon coming my way. Another facet of this gemstone's message is of one's heart's desire—my long-shelved aspiration to write about gardening and sell products and seeds that my garden produced in addition to my work with gemstones.

There was no good reason not to follow my heart's desire. I was simply stuck in a rut I'd never questioned. I'd allowed myself to be sidelined by habit and inertia. I felt that **Rhodonite** was telling me to follow my heart's desire and that a gift or boon would soon be coming my way!

The conflict with the editor may simply have been the Universe's way of letting me know it was time for a change. My self-reading not only addressed my editorial dilemma but made me aware that it was time to enter a new phase of life.

The other group of three stones in the layout was:

Snowflake Obsidian—balance of opposing energies
Turquoise—peace of mind after a period of upheaval
Magnesite—karma or grace.

I interpreted **Snowflake Obsidian** and **Turquoise** to be advising me that by following the advice of the first six stones, I would be moving into a more balanced and peaceful situation replacing the condition of conflict and disturbance. The second **Magnesite** appeared to indicate that grace, or karma, would aid in following my heart's desire. Perhaps it was part of my unfolding destiny to begin writing about my garden.

Following the advice of my self-reading I wrote my first garden-related article which was published soon after submission—a delightful boon as it turns out! Late in 2004 I began marketing garden products and seeds on-line. Thanks to mineral wisdom I'm well on my way to accomplishing my heart's desire.

My self-reading urged me to create needed change more quickly than I would have without the advice of the gemstones. Had I not had the guidance of the reading, I might have lingered longer in an untenable situation missing an important opportunity with a new publication and earning income from my garden through the sale of dried herbs and seeds.

By placing myself in harmony with needed change I found the courage to release the old and embrace a new direction. Acting on the advice in my self-reading the changes I needed occurred quickly and in a positive, favorable manner.

Your own self-readings will alert you to associations and conditions no longer serving your personal growth. I'm not always aware when it's time to let go or move into a new phase. My self-readings help me recognize when changing energy patterns herald an influx of new opportunities.

SELF-READING #2

Another self-reading (below), regarding news and an unexpected gift or windfall was recorded on April of 2006.

This reading revealed what appeared to be two related groups of stones. The first group consisted of:

Labradorite—news coming from a distance.
Serpentine—longtime or primary relationship.
Sunstone—joy, delight.
Rhodonite—an unexpected surprise or boon, heart's desire.
Lined Agate—conflict, disturbance.
Turquoise—peace coming after a period of turmoil.

April 15, 2006 Self-reading

I interpreted this to mean that delight would follow upon a message from afar from someone with whom I had a primary or longtime relationship. The message would likely be, or bring news of a boon or surprise. While the news would bring joy or delight, there would be some element of conflict or disturbance associated with it. However, as **Lined Agate** and **Turquoise** were touching I saw that my "conflict" would be short lived and that I would quickly come to "peace" with the issue.

The next group of stones was:

Pink Aventurine—trusted advisor, mentor.
Sodalite—intuition, following instincts, inner wisdom.
Tiger Eye—a positive outcome despite negative appearances.

THE SELF-READING AND GEMSTONE INTERPRETATION 87

I read these to mean that by following the advice of a trusted advisor or mentor and following my own instincts I could expect a positive outcome despite negative appearances.

A few days following the reading my father, who lives in California, phoned me—my message from someone well known to me at a distance away—and made me an offer. He wanted to send me some old gold and oil stock certificates he had inherited from the estate of my grandfather. His intention was for me to sell them on eBay®. For my effort he would split the proceeds with me.

A degree of conflict and disturbance—**Lined Agate**—arose for me because I had hoped to inherit these certificates as a memento of my grandfather. As the issuing companies were defunct the certificates had no stock value, only sentimental worth and whatever monetary merit attributed to old documents by collectors.

I sought advice from a trusted adviser—**Pink Aventurine**—who suggested going ahead with my father's desires to sell the certificates. I followed the advice and was successful in selling all the certificates very quickly. My gold prospecting instincts—**Sodalite**—came into play when I determined the dollar amount at which to list the certificates. My unexpected gift—**Rhodonite**—was the unanticipated windfall of prosperity coming out of the blue in the form of several hundred dollars—resulting from the sale. **Tiger Eye** indeed predicted a successful, prosperous outcome although initially I'd had mixed feelings regarding my father's offer.

SELF-READING #3

A self-reading from April of 1997 (shown on the next page) predicted betrayal by a female friend. Because of the reading I was aware that the situation was on the horizon. Although, I was unable to prevent it, and didn't know the identity of the "betrayer" until after the fact, knowing it was coming saved me from being as stunned and shocked as I would have been if it had occurred without any warning.

This reading unfolded as follows:

Pyrite (two of them)—betrayal or deception.
Apache Tear—sadness, depression, "tears."
Malachite—the need to be on guard or protect oneself.
Moonstone—female or woman.

Serpentine—someone well known.
Lined Agate—conflict and disturbance.

The upper (North) group of seven stones indicated that major betrayal and deception would manifest. I was advised regarding protection and the need to be on guard. Sadness and "tears" were predicted regarding this issue, which appeared to be a relationship concerning a female well known to me. Conflict and disturbance, possibly even an element of the fear that often underlies conflicts were part of the issue.

Notice how in the illustration of this reading the six stones surrounding Moonstone add layers of meaning? I saw that I was soon to have big trouble with a primary female relationship.

Two stones formed their own group toward the bottom (South) of the pad:

Rose Quartz—healing.
Turquoise—peace coming after a time of trouble.

My interpretation of these stones was that although the event would be painful, healing and peace would follow.

Indeed, the predicted betrayal did occur by a female friend not long after the reading. I suffered all the "tears" indicated by the reading. As to the element of "fear" that sometimes underlies conflict of any kind, I did not feel it was mine but belonged to the woman instigating the trouble. What that fear might be I did not know. Perhaps precise knowledge of what the fear might be attributed to wasn't necessary. I only needed to know that it was a factor in trying to understand to some small degree what had happened.

THE SELF-READING AND GEMSTONE INTERPRETATION

Healing and eventual peace of mind followed that included a new friendship formed with an acquaintance betrayed simultaneously by the same former friend! In our mutual effort to understand what had happened to both of us, we talked things over and discovered we had a lot in common. Although we never figured out why we had both been repudiated we developed a close friendship that exists to this day.

SELF-READING #4

A self-reading dated July 28, 1997, predicted that I would relocate before I had any notion that a move was in my future. The upper group of six gemstones was interpreted as follows:

Sunstone—joy and delight
Crazy Lace Agates (two of them)—physical movement, relocation (Remember more than one can add emphasis or mean "sooner.")
Dalmatian Agate—a legal issue or contract.
Pink Aventurine—an advisor or wise mentor.
Turquoise—peace that follows upon a period of turmoil.

July 28, 1998 Self Reading

I saw I would relocate in the near future. I didn't understand this, however, as I had no intention of selling my home or moving. A legal contract or issue of some type was indicated. What did this mean?

I saw that joy and delight were assured and that peace following a period of turmoil would be achieved. A "mentor" would play a part.

The lower group of three stones appeared to continue the issue of moving.

Crazy Lace Agate (again!)—relocation or move.
Unakite—tension and anxiety
Tiger Eye—success, despite negative appearances to the contrary.

These stones (South end of the pad) were interpreted to mean that the relocation, or move, would result in a period of tension or anxiety but resolve positively despite negative appearances. I didn't know what to make of this self-reading so I simply recorded it. Events predicted by the stones unfolded within a short time.

Three months after the reading, my mother (wise mentor, as it turns out) and I took a trip to Colorado. We passed through Utah on the way and were smitten with the natural wonders and scenic vistas. We arrived in Colorado and enjoyed our vacation although we kept talking about how much we liked Utah.

On our way back home, we stopped again in Utah and on a whim contacted a real estate agent who showed us a couple of lovely homes which were very attractive in a number of ways, including price.

After arriving home to California, again on a whim—just to see what my condo was worth—I contacted another agent to get an idea what I might be able to sell for. I was pleasantly delighted as the sale of my condo would cover purchase of the Utah home and pay for movers too. My mom suggested we jump at the opportunity to move. We listed our condos and mine sold within two weeks. I had my answer; the legal issues indicated by my reading were surely the escrow and other contractual papers having to do with the purchase and sale of two homes and my relocation!

After the escrow on my condo had finalized a check would be wired to Utah for the purchase of the new home. Hearing that all was in order and the money on the way I took off for Utah with a restless cat in the car and the moving van somewhere behind. I arrived in Utah on New Years Eve—December 31, 1997.

The following day I got a phone call that a problem had developed with the escrow on my condo and that it wasn't closed after all—trouble with a paper that had not been submitted and just now discovered!

This news caused a great deal of anxiety, as I wouldn't have the money to purchase the Utah home. Should I call the movers and go back to California? Should I look for a new job fast? I was in Utah with my worldly goods in storage, an antsy cat that wouldn't come out from under the motel bed, and not much money. I may have to try again to sell, or rent my condo. Meanwhile, I'm stuck in a motel with boxes of stuff in storage. Not knowing what to do I did nothing except stay put and worry. Nor could I consult my crystals and gemstones for information. I had packed them in a box with other personal items and they were somewhere in storage with the rest of my worldly goods. I learned a valuable lesson. Always, when traveling, keep your crystals and gemstones near at hand in your overnight bag or, if flying, in your carryon luggage.

Good news finally arrived after a long, stress-filled week. Another phone call came in, this time telling me that the condo's escrow had closed successfully and that the money was finally on the way!

Things did turn out successfully despite negative appearances and a lot of tension and anxiety on my part. However, as the reading promised peace did follow my mental and emotional turmoil. My crystal and gemstone reading had predicted my relocation to Utah even though at the time of the reading I had no plans to move.

SELF-READING #5

The following reading (see illustration on next page) concerns restitution of money from a former boss.

After moving to Utah I took a part-time job in a pottery shop where other employees and I painted decorative pottery. The job was fun and easy and brought in a bit of extra money.

After receiving our paychecks one evening—oddly, in a sealed envelope—several of us went to the market to cash them. Opening our envelopes we discovered that we had been seriously underpaid. Those employees who took theirs to the bank discovered they too had been underpaid and that there were no funds to cover their paychecks, which, of course, bounced! Unable to get satisfaction and money owed from the boss we sought restitution. We filed with the State's employee's resolution board and a hearing was scheduled. Prior to the hearing I did a self-reading.

Apache Tear—feelings of sadness, "tears," and despair.
Lined Agate—conflict.
Pyrite—deception, falsehood.

CRYSTAL AND GEMSTONE DIVINATION

April 4, 1999 Self-reading

Stones shown (top to bottom): Apache Tear, Pyrite, Lined Agate, Rhodonite, Sunstone, Lined Agate, Labradorite, Turquoise, Snowflake Obsidian.

These three stones comprised the upper group of the layout, and I interpreted **Pyrite** as a message regarding the deception by our former boss. **Apache Tear** spoke of the despair and hopeless feelings of the cheated employees, some of whom needed restitution to feed their families and pay bills. The "conflict" addressed by **Lined Agate** was interpreted as the hearing wherein our strife with the boss was to be arbitrated.

Located on the South end of the pad—which I often read as meaning "after" or a "result of"—was another grouping of the following stones:

Labradorite—news from a distance.
Rhodonite—heart's desire.
Snowflake Obsidian—balance of opposites.
Sunstone—a sunny outcome, joy and delight.
Turquoise—peace that follows a period of trouble.
Lined Agate—conflict and disturbance.

The second group of stones—**Labradorite**—foretold of news coming from a distance, while **Sunstone** and **Rhodonite** promised joy and delight, and a pleasant surprise or boon or heart's desire. I took this to mean a positive outcome and restitution of funds. Balance—**Snowflake Obsidian**—would be restored. **Turquoise** suggested a return to peace after our time of turmoil and uncertainty.

We arrived at the hearing, as did our former boss. There was conflict from the start with accusations all around and very negative feelings between employees and former boss. After hearing all sides of the issue the arbitrator dismissed us. We would be informed as to the results of the hearing at a later date.

Within a couple of weeks we all got letters—our news from a distance—informing us that the arbitration had been settled in our behalf. Some of us went out to lunch to celebrate our joy at receiving restitution (balance) of both wages and bounced check fees. The resolution of this case ended our deceptive relationship—**Pyrite**—with the former boss.

As time passes you will marvel at the insights and predictions your self-readings provide. You will also notice that varied issues depicted by the same stones occur again and again. Overtime you may observe that you are dealing in life with the same types of problems on a recurrent basis although the people and circumstances may vary. It seems that in this lifetime I am to learn lessons regarding deceptive relationships!

Recurring themes are one of the ways gemstone wisdom guides you to knowledge of your particular life lesson. While in many of my readings gemstone configuration results in two groupings of stones, this is not something I strive for when I select and lay them on the pad. My eyes are closed during the self-reading selection process and I merely place the stones randomly on the pad. By no means should you try to determine the patterns of the stones on the pad. How they are laid down is part of the mystery and wonder of mineral wisdom! I am continually amazed at what the crystal and gemstone readings tell me even if I cannot always fathom how information revealed in a reading will eventually manifest.

> Whether or not you go on to give readings for others, or simply utilize the crystals and gemstones as tools for self-transformation, your self-readings will prove an invaluable aid when charting your course through life.

The Self-reading and Personal Transformation

As you work with self-readings go slowly and be receptive to each stone you select and how it is positioned on the pad—with others or alone. Listen with your "mind's ear" to any message a stone may relate beyond what you have learned about its basic meaning. Refer back to your readings as time passes and record how events unfolded in relation to the gemstone messages and how you interpreted them. This will help hone your reading skills. You will begin to notice trends and cycles as particular stones keep reappearing in your readings.

As your connection with your crystals and gemstones deepens, the stones may present interesting variations of their primary messages that are tailored to the specifics of your own life or that of anyone you read for. Always take a moment to record any new perspectives or nuances of primary messages as they arise so you won't forget them. The mineral world is beginning to communicate with you on new and deeper levels!

In addition to my self-readings journals, I keep a small notebook in which each stone and its basic message are listed on a page. Here I jot down any newly revealed messages or relevant information under a "notes" heading.

These supplementary messages may be incorporated into your readings if they *feel* applicable to you or a particular querist during a reading.

The crystals and gemstones will let you know which facet of a message is important at the time. You may have a feeling, see an image, possibly "hear," or in some other

In a notebook I record each stone's meaning. In a "Notes" section I record new or interesting information regarding each stone.

manner know what aspect of a message is appropriate. One variation of a message will seem to stand out and you may temporarily "forget" or be unable to recall any other until after the reading.

You may experience during a self-reading an answer you don't like. Perhaps it is not the answer you wanted or expected, so stones are returned to the tray and the question repeated. Again, a negative answer appears.

Does she/he love me-type questions (especially if the stones answer in the negative) are a type of repetitive question likely to be asked. It has been my experience that after a question has been answered two or three times the crystals and gemstones "grow weary" or "turn off" and the results become disconnected, meaningless messages making no sense.

If an answer appears that is distressing or in some way not what is hoped for, instead of re-asking the same question, simply ask, using a three-stone layout, how you might mitigate or offset in some manner the predicted outcome.

I believe that the self-reading is one of the finest of tools for self-transformation. In times of spiritual, physical, or emotional stress the stones will lead you through the mystical desert of your own psyche. I have come to rely on their guidance and wisdom when undergoing challenges, conflict, and indecision.

> Rest assured that this guidance from the mineral realm is available to you!

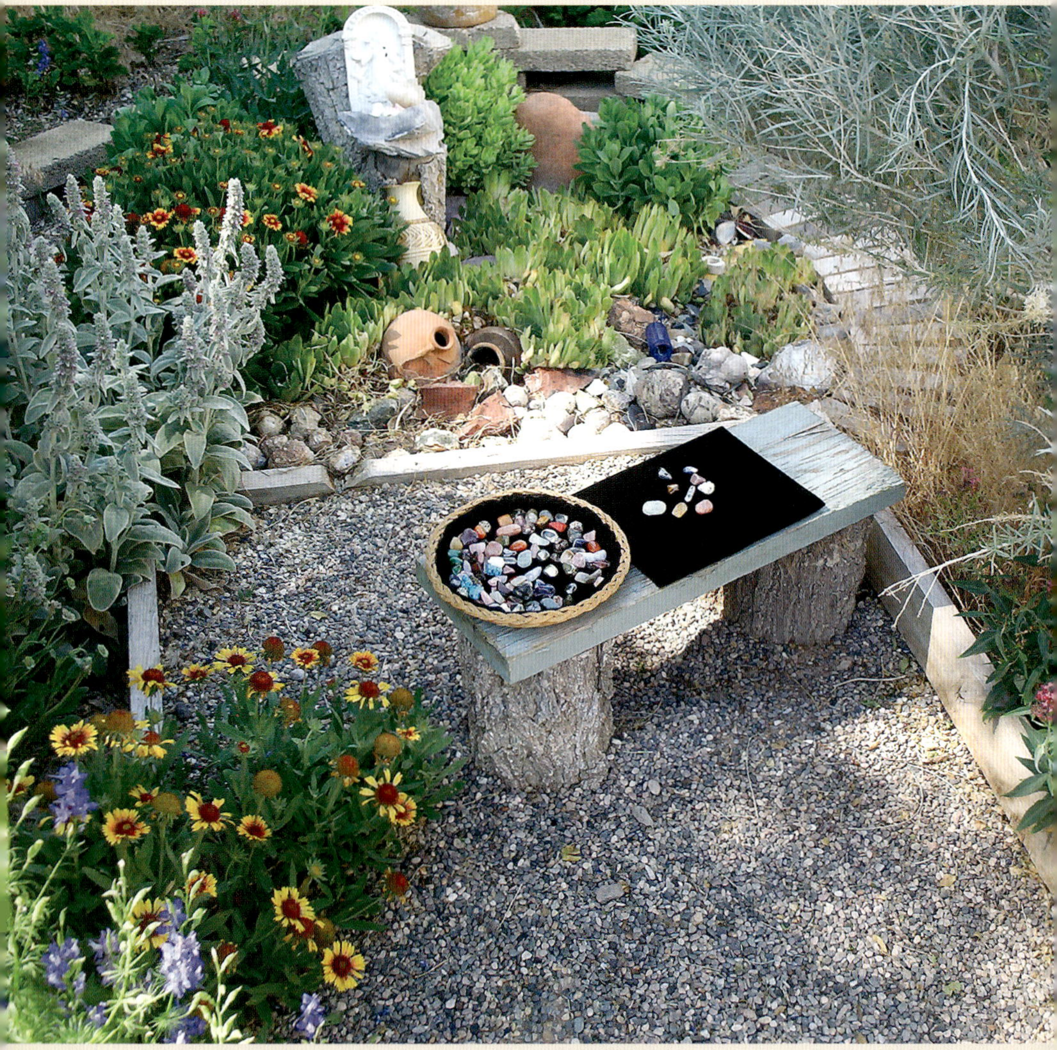

CHAPTER 5

Reading Crystals and Gemstones for Others

ONCE YOU FEEL PROFICIENT INTERPRETING CRYSTAL AND GEMSTONE SELF-READINGS you are likely to be asked by friends and relatives to give them readings too. This is the next natural step that is likely to precede giving readings to clients. It is not a step you need to take unless you feel called to do so. Giving readings for family and friends provides the advantage of immediate and honest feedback on how the readings "felt." You will also get input as to how predicted events unfolded. Giving readings to people you already know and trust will give you the confidence you need should you decide to give readings for the public sector.

In giving readings to others you are joined in the bonds of service with the mineral realm. By giving readings to others you accelerate and expand evolution one individual at a time. For its part, the mineral realm will quicken your own development while at the same time aid you in abetting and accomplishing your desire to be of benefit to others.

Not long after receiving revelations from the mineral realm about this particular method of crystal and gemstone divination I felt called to provide readings for others. I was unsure about this but felt strongly directed by the mineral realm to go forward with this endeavor.

> Remember, one of the purposes of the mineral realm is to aid in the evolution of Earth and all life upon it—humans too—especially humans as we have such a major potential to aid evolution in a positive manner, or be a damaging influence.

I worried about inviting strangers into my home, about my ability to read for others and how much to charge even though I knew that energy needed to be exchanged in some form.

I began advertising via flyers in New Age stores and by word of mouth. I advertised in local newspapers and gave readings at Renaissance Fairs. Eventually I no longer needed to advertise. Word got around and soon I nearly had another full-time job giving readings. I worked at my income-earning job by day and spent evenings and weekends interpreting the messages of crystals and gemstones for others.

For the first few years I kept a bowl near the door and simply allowed querists to donate whatever their conscious dictated. After a time I set a base rate. If a querist wanted, or felt compelled, he or she could contribute additional energy in the form of more money or a service but there was never any pressure to do so. Beyond the base rate I left monetary amounts to the querists' own conscience and perceptions of "value received."

In this chapter I'd like to share with you some of the readings I've recorded for querists over the years. For privacy's sake I won't reveal names. Instead, I will use initials to protect identities. Gender will be disclosed to give clarity to the reading. By sharing these readings I believe it will help familiarize you with the methods and techniques used to interpret what crystals and gemstones have to say and how they express it. Whether you go on to give readings to others, or not, the information in this chapter will aid you in further developing your ability to interpret messages arising out of the mineral realm. The mere fact that you are communicating with crystals and gemstones resonates on etheric and mystical levels and all humans are benefited thereby.

Libbie (right) of Country Mile Farm receives an outdoor reading. I'm relaying the messages of the crystals and gemstones Libbie selected in her nine-stone layout.

When giving a reading to another, I usually don't state the name of a particular stone as I relate its message unless the querist asks me to. The querist will receive a written chronicle of the reading and an illustration bearing the names of the stones for future reference.

During the reading most querists are more interested in the messages the stones have to share. Throwing in the names too may be more distracting than helpful.

Reading the Pad

When reading for others it becomes even more important to recognize how stones are placed upon the pad. In a self-reading quite a bit of information is implied because you know your own life. When you read for another, particularly someone unknown to you, every bit of information revealed by the reading becomes essential. The mineral realm will aid you with subtle promptings and supersensory messages when needed but it helps if you can detect as much meaning as possible out of what lies in your visual field.

I call this "reading the pad!"

When reading for another, I place the basket of stones near the querist where he or she can reach them easily. It helps to have reader and querist positioned opposite one another at a table. The pad lies between so it may be easily seen by both.

Placing the pad and basket of stones between reader and querist makes them easy to see and to reach by both.

The edge of the pad nearest the querist is considered the "North of the pad." The edge nearest the reader is the South regardless of the pad's shape. Stones laid out nearest the querist in the North have to do with present and soon-to-manifest issues. Those laid down toward the South end tend to be further in the future and can be the results of events depicted in the North. Stones laid near the Center of the pad often have to do with issues of greatest concern to the querist. While this directional relationship is not a hard and fast rule it tends to be true much of the time.

The edges of the pad tend to be areas where stones comprising "edge" issues and issues of limited importance may end up. If a querist tends to place unusual numbers of stones along the edge of the mat it may mean that he tends to sideline important issues rather than facing them head on and resolving them.

Stones laid out along the edge of the pad may indicate that the querist tends to sideline important issues rather than dealing with them.

A querist who lays out his stones in a regimented fashion—lining them up or creating rows—may be someone who has a very organized way of conducting life, perhaps to a fault. It can also mean that the querist is looking to create order out of haphazard emotions or issues.

The East of the pad—to the reader's left—may be used to denote new beginnings or cycles in the life of the querist. Stones in this area would indicate issues that may be manifesting soon. The West of the pad—to the right of the reader—can be used to identify emotional trends based upon the gemstones that are set there.

READING CRYSTALS AND GEMSTONES FOR OTHERS 101

The querist who lays stones in rows or lines may be expressing a desire to create order out of chaos or may be someone who is an organizer," and possibly thinks in a regimented manner, or needs to "control" people and things.

Regardless of the shape or orientation of the pad the top edge nearest the querist is the "North" and the edge nearest the reader is the "South."

102   CRYSTAL AND GEMSTONE DIVINATION

In reading the pad I generally use the North and South directions to denote "now" and "soon to be manifesting" respectively, and the Center to keynote immediate concerns. I don't always factor in the East and West significance, as I tend to give more relevance to the gemstone layout, rather than its position on the pad. How much importance you want to give to reading the pad is a choice you as the reader will make. If it helps and applies to your readings do it, if not don't. For me, if reading the pad pops into my head during a reading, it is probably significant that I do so. Other times it doesn't occur to me. I believe that mineral wisdom dictates how much attention I give to the position of stones on the pad.

The following readings are from my files. When giving a reading for someone I sketch the position of stones in a notebook as a basis from which to create a computer-generated illustration that will be emailed to the querist.

Even though I send a computer-generated illustration of a querist's reading, I still make a quick reference sketch during the layouts so I don't forget anything. Here I'm making a quick sketch of Libbie's nine-stone layout.

READING FOR N.Y.

In 1976, shortly after I began to read for others, a querist, whom I'll call N.Y., came for a consultation with the crystals and gemstones.

This querist, a woman, did not initially mention her reason for requesting a reading. She sat nervously picking at her cuticles and fidgeting in her chair as I explained the gemstone selection process.

N.Y. chose nine stones and laid them out as shown in the figure on the next page. I read the upper six-stone group as an indication that she was experiencing an issue

READING CRYSTALS AND GEMSTONES FOR OTHERS 103

N.Y.'s Reading

Blue Lace Agate, Red Jasper, Pyrite, Serpentine, Moonstone, Sodalite, Labradorite, Turquoise, Rose Quartz

with a male well known to her. There appeared to be betrayal involving a woman. I didn't want to come out and tell this woman what the stones were intuiting to me from this layout. What I was seeing was that a husband or boyfriend—**Blue Lace Agate** —or other male close to her— **Serpentine**—was betraying her trust—**Pyrite**—possibly with another woman— **Moonstone**. Red Jasper indicated that passion played a role. I took this to mean a possible sexual affair. **Sodalite** was telling me that the querist herself suspected the likelihood of what was going on.

Even so, I approached this as delicately as I could telling her that betrayal lay at the heart of the issue for which she'd sought the reading. The issue revolved around a male and female in some type of passionate relationship. She burst into tears. I felt awful, as this was one of my first readings for someone I'd never met.

As she sobbed she told me that she was afraid that her husband was having an affair with a woman from his workplace. I didn't feel that it was my place to confirm this part of the reading. I felt it was true and based upon her reaction so did she.

I read that she would soon be receiving news—possibly from a distance— **Labradorite**—from someone, possibly unknown to her, regarding this issue. Greatly relieved that the remainder of the reading gave good news I told her that **Turquoise** indicated that after a period of turmoil she would enter a cycle of peace, contentment, and healing—**Rose Quartz**. She asked what this meant so I directed her to return the nine stones to the basket, and hold her question in her mind as she drew three more stones and laid them on the pad.

N.Y. chose the following three gemstones, **Citrine, Snowflake Obsidian,** and **Dalmatian Agate**. Following up on the messages of **Turquoise** and **Rose Quartz** from the previous layout, I answered her question that a positive new beginning was in her future—**Citrine. Snowflake Obsidian**—balance, or balance of opposites—indicated that it was likely she would be entering a more balanced state, regarding the issue for which she'd sought the reading.

Citrine

Snowflake Ovsidian

Dalmatian Agate

N.Y.'s Question

Snowflake Obsidian may also refer, under certain conditions, to union with the opposite sex. I *felt* that in her case this stone was indicating that she would be entering into a new relationship—possibly including marriage. **Dalmatian Agate**—things of a legal nature and contracts, etc.—appeared in close relationship to **Snowflake Obsidian** and seemed to portend a "marriage" feeling for me.

There were two ways to interpret this layout. First, that divorce—another legal issue covered by **Dalmatian Agate**—would be the means of freeing her from her present situation, allowing her to become open to a new relationship. Or, that marriage would result from her new relationship.

I didn't want to mention the word "divorce" as I felt she wasn't ready to entertain such a possibility. She only "suspected" her husband of misconduct. So I merely answered that **Citrine** heralded a positive "new beginning" of some type and that balance—**Snowflake Obsidian**—would be restored within the context of "a marriage." Whether it was her current relationship or a new one I left to her to work out as I didn't want to upset her by suggesting her present marriage may not be the one referred to in the reading. She was already stressed and upset as it was.

As N.Y. had no further questions I asked if she would like a health reading suggesting that the there could be some useful advice arising from the crystals and gemstones that might help her to cope with her worries. Clearing the pad, I directed her to choose five crystals and/or gemstones that appealed to her in some manner.

Crystals and gemstones alter their primary messages when selected as part of a health reading. They often suggest their own "cure" for messages they bring!

The first stone that N.Y. selected was **Unakite**. Its basic message is one of stress, tension, and emotional and physical pain resulting from issues and events. In a health reading this gemstone advises the need to prioritize and evaluate what is truly important.

Perhaps some items may be delegated, temporarily shelved, or moved to the bottom of a "to-do" list. As a result I advised N.Y. that despite her fears regarding her husband,

and that until she received confirmation, she should try to concentrate on those areas of her life over which she had control—her children, her home and health, and her job.

Pyrite in the context of a health reading advises the querist to take care in the diet. Eat good, healthful food and avoid junk foods. I advised her to watch her diet and eat properly. Although she would continue to fret over her suspicions regarding her husband, she could help prevent potential health issues caused from stress by giving her body nutritious foods.

Sunstone's Life Message advised N.Y. to nourish herself beyond merely eating well. **Moss Agate** indicated that she nurture herself. Relaxing massages, taking long soaks in the tub, getting her hair done, and pampering herself were recommendations that I made to help her to relax and nurture herself. These types of things would aid in reducing the *physical* effects of stress and *temporarily* take her mind off her troubles. Another message of **Moss Agate** in the health portion of the reading continues its overall message of green and growing things. I suggested that N.Y. add walking in a nearby park to her regimen. Walking is soothing, strengthening and stress relieving.

I asked if N.Y. liked to garden and she answered in the affirmative. I suggested she spend time in her garden, possibly adding some new plants or sowing some seeds—additional facets continuing **Moss Agate's** message. Planting and sowing are events by which we invest in our own future and reap the results when plants mature and bear flowers and fruits for our enjoyment. There are healing benefits to be gained by spending time in nature or in outdoor environments.

Rose Quartz assured N.Y. that she would experience healing on some level. A few days later I mailed N.Y. a sketch and typewritten interpretation of her crystal and gemstone reading.

More than two years passed before I heard from N.Y. again. She had moved out of state and was living happily with her children and new husband. She told me that about two months after her reading the woman involved with her ex-husband called her at home and confessed to the relationship. N.Y.'s intuition—**Sodalite**—had been confirmed and she received the message promised by **Labradorite**.

N.Y. confronted her husband and he asked for a divorce to pursue the relationship with his co-worker. N.Y. didn't contest the divorce. She continued to work and began taking night classes to earn a nursing degree to increase her income-earning potential. She ended up taking a job at a hospital in another state, meeting and marrying a prominent physician.

N.Y. told me that although she suffered greatly at the loss of her first marriage, the reading gave her hope during her dark hours that all would be okay in the end. She said the information received in the health reading gave her coping and stress-reduction techniques and helped balance out the turmoil in her life. Nurturing herself allowed her to feel attractive and worthwhile during a time when she felt abandoned and forsaken. I had to admire N.Y. because when feeling at life's lowest ebb it is hard to give oneself ultimate self-care as was advised by her reading. Despite her sadness and depression she adhered to the advice of the reading and came triumphantly through a dark time in her life.

READING FOR F.R.

Following is a reading from 1986 for a querist, whom I'll call F.R. F.R. had concerns about an organization he belonged to. He suspected that the governing body of the organization was mishandling funds *and* creating dissention and discord among the members. F.R. was up front and stated at the outset the reason for his reading. Because F.R.'s issue was a rather unusual one his initial disclosure aided me in my interpretation of the crystal and gemstone messages (see ilustration on next page).

I began by advising F.R. that anything revealed in the reading was purely for informational purposes. He would not be able to use the reading as evidence to confront the officers with any type of legal action. F.R. would have to discover irrefutable physical evidence that there was indeed financial and ethical misconduct in his organization. The reading was *only* for the purposes of guiding him in finding evidence or deciding the course of potential action he might take.

F.R. chose the following nine stones for his initial layout:

Malachite—warning to be on guard or a need for protection
Dalmatian Agate—a legal or contractual issue is in question
Unakite—anxiety, tension, pain, can also mean "burning the candle at both ends" or living a "double life."
Pyrite—betrayal, deception, mistrust
Lined Agate—conflict

The top five stones in the North of the pad I interpreted as follows. **Malachite** indicated that there was indeed something to be alert or on guard about and a need for protection. The proximity of **Dalmatian Agate** spoke of a legal contract, by-laws, or agreement of some type—I interpreted this as the issue at risk, and needing protection. **Pyrite** indicated that betrayal and deception and reason for mistrust did indeed exist.

As F.R. had already revealed that the officers in question seemed to be sowing chaos among the membership, I felt that **Lined Agate** and **Unakite** were addressing this aspect of the issue and that the reason why anyone was sowing discord or conflict among the membership may be revealed as the reading proceeded.

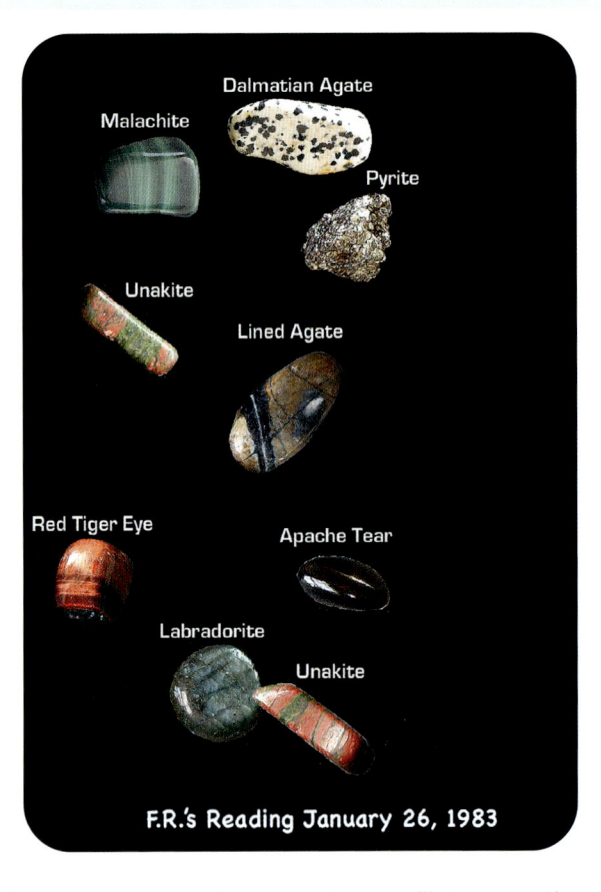

> **Red Tiger Eye**— perfectionist, ego, expecting too much of self. I intuited a "Type-A" personality.
> **Apache Tear**—despair, "tears," despondency, a negative situation.
> **Unakite**—stress, tension, anxiety, can also mean burning the candle at both ends or living a double life.

I related to F.R. that someone with an elevated ego, possibly a perfectionist-type—someone picky about detail—was involved and that this person was an anxious, tense

READING CRYSTALS AND GEMSTONES FOR OTHERS 109

person—possibly "living a double life" were the words that popped into my mind. This situation was causing a lot of distress to the **Red Tiger Eye**-person, along with negative feelings, such as despair and despondency revealed by **Apache Tear**.

F.R. indicated that one of the organization's officers fit the description of "perfectionist" and "nitpicker."

Lined Agate seemed to be bridging the first group of stones to the next group. I told F.R. that the conflict being perpetrated among the members might be a factor at the center of two issues and that we could explore this further in the form of a question after finishing the initial layout.

Labradorite—news from a distance or from someone unknown was also indicated. I advised F.R. to be on the lookout for an incoming message that would bring news that might shed more light on the issue within his organization. Because one of the **Unakites** was touching closely upon **Labradorite**, I felt this news would be fraught with tension and anxiety.

After returning the first nine stones to the basket F.R. drew three more to ask a question to clarify more about the causes underlying the potential misconduct.

This layout (at the left) revealed more information as to the reason why the misconduct was occurring.

Turritella Agate (two of them) usually regards an increase of money. More than one often indicates a *need* for money.

Turritella Agate
Moonstone
Turritella Agate

F.R.'s Question

CRYSTAL AND GEMSTONE DIVINATION

Moonstone—a female or woman.

This could be the reason for the misconduct! A woman seemed to be at the heart of a need for money. I related my interpretation to the querist. I added that the **Pyrite** from his previous layout might not only be referring to betrayal to the organization, but that it might be a theme carrying throughout the issue of suspected misconduct.

F.R. drew another three stones for his second question (see the illustration on the right).

Red Jasper—passion, usually with a sexual component
Pyrite—betrayal, mistrust
Turritella Agate—increase in money...again

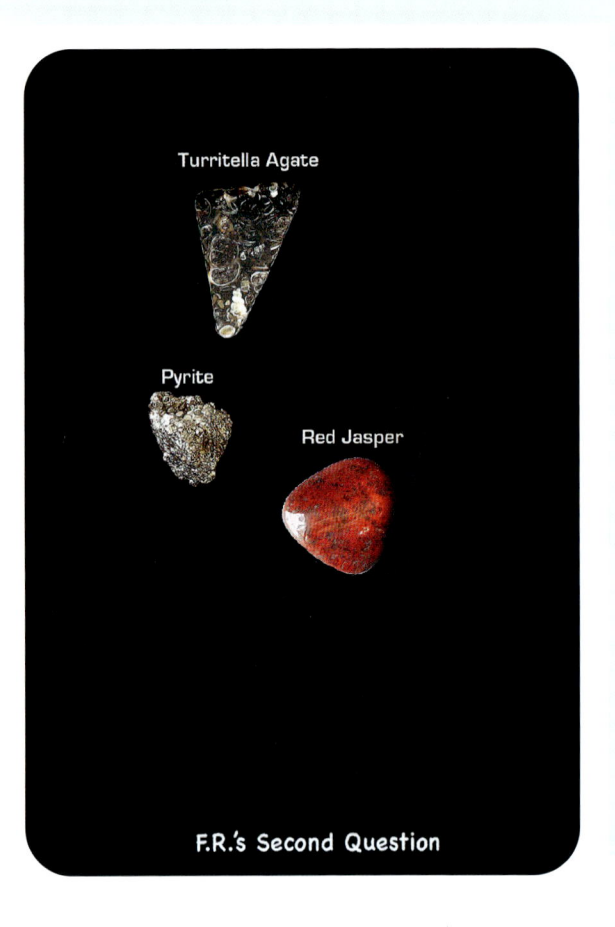

F.R.'s Second Question

Taking into consideration what the first question revealed and that this second three-stone layout was for the purpose of gaining more insight, I interpreted this answer (see illustration above) as a love affair that may have gone badly and that somehow money was an issue. Was it possible that a woman scorned was blackmailing an officer of the organization? Or, had he gotten in trouble financially trying to provide monetarily for this woman? The occurrence of Turritella Agate again in answer to the second question appeared to continue the theme of "money," or a "need for money" rather than its usual meaning of *increased* money. I related the potentials to F.R.

F.R. declined the health portion of the reading indicating that he had gained sufficient leads to set him on his way to gathering more information.

A few months later F.R. sent me a clipping of an article that appeared in his local newspaper revealing that an officer—a man well-known in his community and high up in a prominent charitable organization—had been having a love affair with a woman. The officer decided he wanted to break off the affair. The woman, however, threatened to reveal the liaison to the officer's wife and family and to expose the details publicly, as well. In order to protect family and reputation the man began pilfering small amounts of funds from the organization as hush money. A little became more, and eventually the treasurer of the organization became suspicious and phoned the querist (the "anxious news from a distance" promised by **Labradorite** and **Unakite**) with proof of what was going on, and together with other officers brought the issue to justice. The conflict and chaos loosed among the organization's members had indeed been an effort by the troubled officer to misdirect attention.

> Remember that it is not up to the reader to give legal or relationship advice. A reader merely relates "potentials" when interpreting the messages of crystals and gemstones. The querist must verify and act upon the information.

While most issues querists bring to a reading concern family, romance, finances, job, and so on, you will get people coming with unusual, out of the ordinary requests.

READING FOR B.R.

The following reading was sought on an issue regarding a personality change. This querist didn't give so much as a hint as to why she'd requested a reading. This is what I refer to as a "cold reading." The querist is unknown to the reader and provides no initial information as to why a reading is sought. The querist may be testing the reader as to whether there is legitimacy in the service provided or the issue is too personal to relate.

This querist chose (see illustration on next page):

Unakite—tension, anxiety, pain, double life, etc.
Blue Lace Agate—male, brother, father, son, lover.
Red Tiger Eye—ego, perfectionist, Type-A, sometimes intolerance.
Turritella Agate—(two of them) money, need for money (if more than one).
Apache Tear—despair, tears, depression, and negativity.
Bloodstone—troubled but loving relationship.
Lined Agate—conflict and fear.
Sodalite—follow your instincts or intuition.

I interpreted this reading as the central issue being a man—**Blue Lace Agate**—and that the man in question appeared to be a Type A or perfectionist personality—**Red Tiger Eye**. I could see that quite a bit of trouble surrounded him. It appeared he was in need of money—**Turritella Agate** (more than one). And it looked as though a lot of negativity surrounded him, some possibly in the form of despair or depression —**Apache Tear**.

Certainly there appeared to be trouble surrounding a loving but troubled relationship—**Bloodstone**—and anxiety and tension—**Unakite**. Fear and conflict in some form—**Lined Agate** were also issues. As I related these things, the querist volunteered that she was very worried about her older brother. Perhaps the tension and anxiety the reading was picking up belonged to the querist? Or, possibly these feelings belonged to her brother? Maybe both were true.

I advised her that she should be open to her feelings and instincts—**Sodalite**—concerning the issue. B.R. then related that her brother was a successful, businessman (the querist later volunteered that "Type A, perfectionist" described her brother perfectly) who lived a rich lifestyle. Lately, however, he had been asking to borrow money from the querist and other family members. Furthermore, he had become very reclusive and withdrawn. B.R. was worried as she didn't understand what was wrong with her brother and when she asked he denied any problem.

I asked B.R. if she needed further clarification. She indicated that she would like to ask for more specifics as to what might be wrong. Instead of directing her to draw three stones in response to her question, I had the feeling she should draw five and directed her to return the nine-stone layout to the basket, visualize her question and draw five more stones. The five stones she drew were:

B.R.'s First Question

Lined Agate —(two of them) conflict, disturbance, fear
Unakite—stress, tension, pain.
Amegreen—transformational energy
Apache Tear—depression, despair, tears, negativity

Of the five stones selected, only one had a possibly positive connotation—**Amegreen**. However, as stones with negative messages of pain, conflict, fear, tension, despair and depression surrounded this gemstone, I felt that the transformation spoken of would be negative rather than positive. I told B.R.

what the gemstones were relaying and that these things were likely causing the personality changes she was witnessing.

B.R. wanted to ask another question so I directed her as before.

This time she selected:

Unakite—(two of them) tension, anxiety, possibly burning the candle at both ends.
Lined Agate—(two of them) conflict, perhaps fear.
Fossilized Dinosaur Bone—change in one's job situation.

By now I was beginning to realize that **Lined Agate** had come up in each layout and that an ongoing theme of conflict and fear—**Lined Agate**, and tension and anxiety—**Unakite** were in serious play around B.R.'s brother. Too, because she was worried about him, she was experiencing these emotions, as well, intensifying these messages from the mineral realm.

I didn't ask what B.R.'s second question was but related the gemstone messages as I saw them in her five-stone layout. I told her that in addition to tension and anxiety, it was possible that her brother might be "burning his candle at both ends" or that he was living a double life—**Unakite**. More than one **Unakite** in this layout seemed to be expanding upon its message. Possibly one "life" was a "public" persona; the

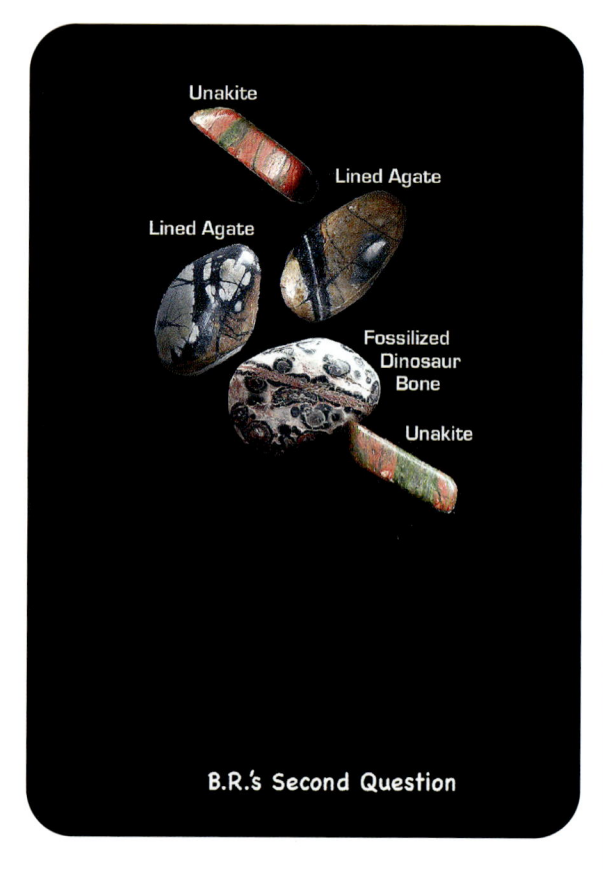

READING CRYSTALS AND GEMSTONES FOR OTHERS 115

other might be an aspect he kept hidden from family and coworkers. It appeared that there could possibly be conflict—**Lined Agates—**on the work front—**Petrified Dinosaur Bone**—as these three stones were in close proximity. Anxiety and tension were impinging on the work front because of the **Unakite** and **Fossilized Dinosaur Bone** overlap.

I "felt" that due to the trouble surrounding the brother's work situation he might have lost his job, or soon would be. That might explain why he was attempting to borrow money from the querist and other family members.

B.R. indicated that she didn't need to ask any further questions. I asked if she wanted a health reading and she asked if I could do one for her brother instead. Although the querist's brother was not present, I've done birthday readings for friends and relatives living out of state. One's presence is not required and distance is not an issue.

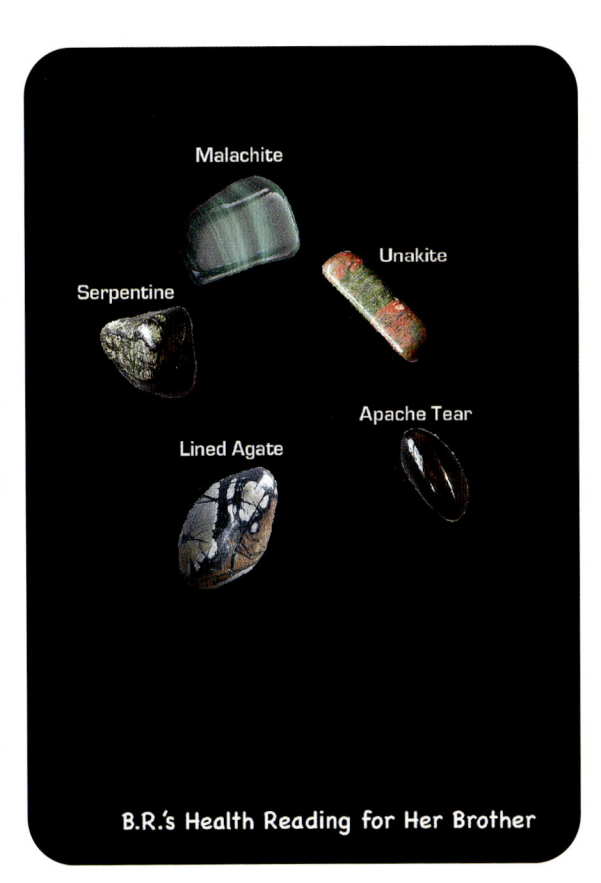

I agreed that this was possible and asked B.R. to visualize her brother and silently ask regarding his health as she drew five gemstones for the health reading. Remember that in the health portion of the reading the primary mineral messages don't usually apply, but alter their character to address health issues.

She drew:

Malachite—guard the immune system immune-enhancing herbs may be indicated.
Unakite—anxiety, tension, pain, the need to prioritize.
Serpentine—addiction or compulsion.

B.R.'s Health Reading for Her Brother

Lined Agate—digestion, a possible need for dark green foods or digestive herbs.
Apache Tear—warning that a situation should be avoided or a severe lack or deficiency is impending.

I noticed that Apache Tear had been selected again, although in a health reading its message changes. By now I was beginning to think that the querist's worry and anxiety for her brother was coming through every aspect of the reading—**Unakite**. Not sure, I told her of this possibility. I also indicated that her brother might be suffering from digestive trouble—**Lined Agate**—possibly as a result of the problems going on in his life.

At this point B.R. volunteered that her brother had lost a lot of weight recently and this was an additional cause of worry to the family. I went on to tell her that it appeared he might be suffering some type of compulsion or addiction—**Serpentine.** The mineral realm was indicating strongly—**Malachite**—that if he didn't seek help for his health problems that his immune system could be compromised. I urged B.R. to tell her brother to be extra careful regarding his health. The Serpentine troubled me greatly and I told her so. Particularly disturbing was this stone's message of "addiction."

From the standpoint of the other layouts it looked potentially as if B.R.'s brother might be suffering from substance abuse. Burning the candle at both ends, the potential for leading a double life, money problems, sudden weight loss, trouble at work, relationships that are troubled, conflict, negative emotions, etc. are indications of this.

> I really dislike giving a querist bad news. I try to find the right words to soften news of this kind, and this was such a case. I gently and reluctantly told her that it was possible that her brother's compulsion or addiction might be drug or substance related.

B.R. confessed that she did indeed have a feeling—**Sodalite** (from her nine-stone layout) that drug addiction might be the root cause. The first layout had confirmed to her that her suspicions were correct when I advised that she follow her intuition!

Although B.R. eventually became a regular client, she never again brought up the subject of her brother and I didn't ask. A querist's privacy is of utmost importance and she chose not to address the subject further.

READING FOR L.M.

The next querist, L.M., came to see me from the southern desert area of California. She was concerned about the number of earthquakes that were occurring on a daily basis.

L.M. had spoken with someone from a geological center and had not received information that allayed her fear and concern. A geologist had told her that the clusters of earthquakes might be a precursor for a large quake—and after all, the area was long overdue for a "Big One." Not a comforting thought!

I found this reading interesting because it was the only one I've ever given where a querist was consulting the mineral realm on a question directly related to that realm rather than on issues of a personal nature. Who but the mineral realm would really be able to give this querist an answer that wasn't a guess or a "might be"!

L.M. drew the following stones:

Lined Agate—conflict
Unakite—stress, tension, pain
Apache Tear—despair, depression, tears, a negative situation
Moss Agate—Nature, green and growing things.
Sodalite—inner wisdom, intuition, instincts
Snowflake Obsidian—balance, sometimes union
Rose Quartz—healing.
Turquoise—return to peace after a period of upheaval
Tiger Eye—a positive outcome despite appearances to the contrary.

L.M.'s Earthquake Reading September 3, 2005

This might have been a hard reading to give "cold" if the querist had not shared her issue of concern. I may have assumed a personal or financial issue instead of a geologic concern! Merely knowing that L.M.'s matter was not of the human realm enabled me to connect with the stones in a different manner than I usually do. As a result I read and received intuitively information from the mineral realm that was more surprising to me than to the querist! Based upon the layout *and* tuning into the energy of the gemstones selected, I read the stones in the following manner:

I "saw" that there was conflict—**Lined Agate**—in the energy between the human and mineral realms in desert communities outside San Diego. The problem was due to a rapid build up of population and the resulting construction projects that were occurring so rapidly that the Earth forces could not maintain balance.

The building of strip malls, roadways, and housing subdivisions were all disrupting the normal flow of Earth-energy—**Moss Agate**—on a massive scale. Too, a great deal of stress—**Unakite**—had built up in the ground as a result of the ongoing movement of two continental plates sliding slowly past one another along the San Andreas Fault. Several minor faults connected to the San Andreas were being used to redirect energy away from the larger fault via a series of low magnitude quakes.

The manmade imbalance and natural buildup of geologic stress had put a significant strain upon the surrounding land resulting in an extremely negative—**Apache Tear**—situation. The "wisdom"—**Sodalite**—of Nature—**Moss Agate**—in an effort to balance—**Snowflake Obsidian**—the situation was the root cause of the earthquake clusters. This was occurring in order to prevent major breakage along the San Andreas that would potentially result in catastrophic destruction and major loss of life.

I further understood that prevention, by the mineral realm, of a large earthquake along the San Andreas Fault would continue for as long as possible via smaller faults along its north-south axis. There would, however, come a time when such preventative measures would fail.

> The day would come when the mineral realm would no longer be able to redirect a buildup of negative energy, and the San Andreas Fault would be the source of a major earthquake somewhere along its length. Negative energy was building but thus far the mineral realm had been able to offset the worst-case effects.

READING CRYSTALS AND GEMSTONES FOR OTHERS 119

The reading went on to let the querist know that the current earthquake clusters would heal—**Rose Quartz**—the immediate problem and that peace would again be restored to the land after a period of turmoil—**Turquoise.**

The mineral realm was assuring the querist that although the earthquake clusters were disturbing and frightening, the immediate outcome would be positive—**Tiger Eye**—despite present unsettling appearances.

L.M.'s health reading consisted of the following five stones:

Sodalite—pay attention to intuition and dreams.
Turritella Agate—kidneys, bladder, urinary tract.
Lepidolite— letting go, releasing.
Red Tiger Eye—the need to relax and nurture oneself.
Girasol—need to drink water or add it into the environment.

I advised L.M. that she needed to pay attention to her intuition and images seen in her dreams—**Sodalite**—and meditations and that it appeared that she was or would be having issues concerning either her kidneys and/or bladder—**Turritella Agate.**

At this L.M. laughed and told me that she was currently taking antibiotics for a chronic bladder infection that would clear up and then return. She explained that she had laughed because for some time she had been having dreams of being in

L.M.'s Health Reading

public places, such as malls or churches, and having to urinate very badly. In her dreams she was always trying to find a spot out of public view where she could relieve herself.

The reading went on to suggest that there was something she needed to let go of —**Lepidolite**—and in doing so would, at last, find relief from her infection.

I told her that resentment or anger at a situation or person was often an issue surrounding urinary tract infections. I advised L.M. to search her heart and mind for anything that she might be holding on to. Forgiveness is one of the most effective methods for relieving longstanding anger or resentment.

Red Tiger Eye advised L.M. to relax and take time for herself—not to take life so seriously. **Girasol** was very practical in its appearance because it advised her to drink more water, which we both agreed, was very practical advice for someone with a bladder infection!

READING FOR B.L.

The next example from my files concerns a young man, the son of a friend of mine, who lives several hundred miles away. He wanted me to do a long distance reading for him.

B.L.'s concern was that he hadn't met that "special someone." B.L. didn't frequent bars or clubs. He wasn't someone who dated casually, yet he desperately wanted to meet a lovely young woman.

B.L. tended to be somewhat of a loner, loath to play the dating game, and opposed to dating services. Other than the workplace (most of the employees were men) he felt he had no hope of meeting a young woman with whom he could marry and settle down.

Holding B.L. in mind, I closed my eyes and selected nine stones on his behalf since he would not be present for his reading.

The stones I selected were:

Amegreen—Life changing transformation.
Moss Agate—Nature, green and growing things.
Moonstone—female energy, woman or girl, sister, spouse, etc.
Sunstone—joy and delight.
Magnesite—fate, karma, grace.

Lined Agate— conflict, sometimes fear.
Red Tiger Eye—ego, perfectionism, intolerance.
Lepidolite—letting go of something no longer needed.
Unakite—tension, anxiety, pain, etc.

This reading seemed to be addressing two issues. In the South of the pad were stones that seemed to relate to B.L.'s issue of concern—meeting a young woman. **Amegreen** spoke of life-changing transformation that could be karmic in scope—**Magnesite**. **Amegreen** told me that B.L.'s life, as he has known it for the past decade or so, was about to shift in a dramatic but positive manner as no stones bearing negative messages appeared in this grouping. The proximity of **Sunstone** strongly indicated that this shift would be one that would bring joy and delight. Nearby **Moonstone** advised that the energy of a woman would be entering his reality.

B.L.'s Romance Reading October 1, 2000

The presence of **Moss Agate** was a little puzzling. Although it means Nature and green and growing things this stone was partially covering **Moonstone**. These two stones were not only "joined" by physically touching but one lay slightly atop the other. Rather than advising B.L. to get out and enjoy communion with the natural world, I felt that **Moss Agate** was telling me something *about* the female energy soon to enter B.L.'s experience! Somehow this woman had something to do with Nature. Perhaps she was an outdoorsy type, or maybe she was someone who was at ease with Nature or was a "natural" type of person—one without airs. If the last possibility were correct, she would be someone that B.L. would feel right at home with. Perhaps she was indeed the soul mate for which he had been longing!

However, of more immediate concern were the stones in the North portion of the pad. These were "now" issues or those soon to manifest and were closer in the future for B.L. than those foretelling meeting his soul mate. The "North" stones led me to believe that a separate, negative issue was being addressed.

Lepidolite was indicating that there was something or someone in B.L.'s life that had run its course and it was time to let it let go. **Red Tiger Eye** spoke of someone with an ego, a need for perfection sometimes to the point of being intolerable or intolerant. I didn't feel that this related to either B.L. or the feminine energy indicated in the first group of stones.

I could see that **Unakite**, **Lepidolite**, and **Lined Agate** appeared to "embrace" or "cup" **Red Tiger Eye**. It looked to me that the stones in close proximity to **Red Tiger Eye** were advising of a relationship fraught with stress, anxiety, and conflict that should be released. It appeared to me that B.L. was being advised to let this other relationship go! As I knew that B.L.'s life consisted mostly of work at the time of the reading, I felt that this meant he was having trouble with someone at work.

B.L. also had requested a health reading as he was having some type of physical trouble that was minor but annoying. I had been unaware that he had any problems and because of his private nature he did not reveal what it was. He wanted to see what the stones had to say in addition to what his physician had prescribed.

Closing my eyes I selected the following five stones for B.L.:

Aquamarine—head, brain, migraines or headaches.
Unakite—stress and the need to prioritize and address the root cause.
Turritella Agate—kidneys, bladder, urinary tract.
Rose Quartz—healing would be experienced.
Girasol—need for water in one's body or environment.

This gemstone layout suggested that B.L. might be suffering from headaches, migraines, or possibly insomnia. Perhaps the **Red Tiger Eye** person at his workplace was a figurative "headache" or that the stress of dealing with this person was actually causing him headaches. At any rate it appeared that **Unakite** was advising that the source of the health issue was stress and anxiety. Because of **Unakite** there was an indication that pain may be part of the health issue. **Unakite** was also advising B.L. that he needed to address the *root cause* of his health problem.

Turritella Agate in the health context of the reading was advising that B.L. might be having some type of urinary tract problem. It appeared that *two* health issues, instead of one, were being addressed by the presence of both **Aquamarine** and **Turritella Agate**.

It is interesting to note that **Aquamarine** lies above in the "head" position while **Turritella Agate** lies below almost as if these stones, with **Unakite** between were forming the map of a body to indicate the locations of B.L.'s health concerns! **Rose Quartz** advised B.L. that healing would occur.

Too, **Girasol** was indicating that B.L. would benefit by either drinking more water or having it in his environment in some manner. Adding the *experience* of water to his life by visiting the ocean, a river, or lake could help ease stress and tension. I doubted he would take this advice as he tended to be a homebody. I advised that taking long soaks in the tub would be a relaxing way to enjoy water at home. However, knowing B.L. as I do it was doubtful he would take long tub soaks, as I knew him to be a "shower person," although a long steamy shower can be very relaxing.

After sending the results of the reading, B.L.'s mother solved the water problem by purchasing a small fountain for his nightstand. Whether B.L. drank more water, as advised, I do not know. Soda pop and Slim Fast are his main beverage choices.

I don't know if the health reading resonated with B.L.'s health problem or not. I did learn that part of the problem was located "below the waist," however; B.L.'s mother did confirm that he was having migraine headaches and suffering from insomnia, as well.

At the time of B.L.'s reading the only portion that was in present time were his problems with his boss. After B.L. received the reading he shared it with his mother and she told me about the boss trouble. It seemed a personality conflict was growing worse. B.L.'s boss was pleased with his work product and wasn't finding fault there, but in other areas there was nagging and bad temper. B.L. was tired of his boss's flash point anger and habit of making demeaning comments about the other employees in the workplace. B.L. was thinking of quitting and looking for other work. Doing so would be in alignment with the mineral wisdom revealed during his reading.

Within months of receiving his reading, the business partner of B.L.'s boss's left and formed his own company offering B.L. a high-level position with better salary. The health problems and stress plaguing B.L. cleared up not long after his job situation improved.

B.L. has since met a lovely, young woman, whom I'll call "N." They began dating several years ago before moving in together. At the time of this writing they are planning their May wedding!

I puzzled over the presence of **Moss Agate** in the reading. Upon meeting N., I had my answer. She is a beautiful young woman, both inwardly and outwardly. N. is also very natural! She wears no makeup. She doesn't need too. N. is equally natural in her temperament and style of dress. I have met her on several occasions when traveling to California and once when she and B.L. came out and stayed as my guests for several days.

● ● ● ● ● ● ●

These examples of readings from my files should give you an idea of some of the types of things to expect when reading for others. Hopefully they will also prepare you for unexpected issues, as well. After reading crystals and gemstones for many years I still am amazed and surprised by information flowing from the mineral realm. I think you, too, will be pleasantly surprised and amazed!

CHAPTER 6

Gemstone Forecasting and Other Divination Systems

You may be reading this book because of an interest in the metaphysical applications of crystals and gemstones and a curiosity about how they are used for divination. Perhaps you already use a divination system such as Tarot cards or Rune Stones and are merely curious about the crystal and gemstone method. Regardless of what drew you to this book, crystal and gemstone divination is a seldom-explored aspect of the mineral realm that combines beautifully with other divination systems. I have found that mineral wisdom coming through crystal and gemstone readings combines with, enhances, and deepens my experience with other systems—in my case Tarot.

A few years ago a dear friend, Teri, gave me the gift of a deck of Tarot cards. She is a proficient intuitive Tarot reader and has long given readings at psychic fairs and for clients coming to her home. Teri taught me to read the cards intuitively rather than by traditional meanings and associations. As I became more proficient in my understanding of Tarot imagery I recognized that particular cards (in the way I read them) resonated with certain crystals and gemstones in my divination collection. While crystal and gemstone readings remain, for me, my preferred method, I have given readings using both gemstones and Tarot. The results of combining the two systems have been illuminating. I believe most divination systems would integrate seamlessly with crystal and gemstone readings.

As I am somewhat familiar with Tarot cards I will make some associations between them and the crystal and gemstone method that may be helpful if you wish to use both systems together.

There are many systems of foretelling and I cannot cover all of them here. Yet, seeing how I have matched the messages of gemstones with those of Tarot, perhaps you will be inspired to meld your present system and crystal and gemstone divination.

I do not claim to be an expert Tarot reader as it takes many years to become proficient and uncover its diverse layers of meaning. The more I learn about the cards the more there is to learn! Yet, I find Tarot's imagery fascinating and intriguing.

I will share what I have discovered and where I have found meaning. If you read the Tarot differently than I, you will be making adjustments to how you match stones to cards. Not only do individual stones resonate with Tarot, you will find that combinations and groups of stones in proximity also echo the meaning of particular cards.

There are a greater number of Tarot cards in a deck than there are stones in the gemstone set. However, there is a harmony of expression between stones and cards. A particular gemstone or crystal may encompass the meaning of more than one card.

I cannot list all the potential combinations as no two Tarot readers see the cards in precisely the same manner. However, following are some possibilities to use as examples, reflect upon, change, or add to them as best suits your purpose and how *you* define the cards.

Tarot card readings blend harmoniously with gemstone and crystal readings.

AMEGREEN

Transformation! One aspect of this gemstone is in The Tower. Amegreen suggests "big change" that is life altering or affects one on several levels simultaneously—physical, spiritual, and emotional. The Tower carries a message of sudden, transformative change and upheaval often negative, not always. Amegreen also carries this message; however, Amegreen tells us that that change, while sudden and threatening, may also be positive in nature.

AMETHYST

This crystal always resonates with spiritual matters. There are several Tarot cards that reflect the wisdom of this gemstone. The Hierophant, Ace of Swords, and Ace of Cups are three cards that come immediately to mind.

The alchemical imagery of the Ace of Swords is that of Kundalini energy. From the spirit hand (coiled serpent in Eastern mysticism) Kundalini, or serpent energy, rises upwards along the spine (depicted by the sword) to the crown chakra represented by the foliage-garlanded crown.

The Ace of Cups' mystical imagery speaks of the descent of Spirit energy (as a dove) that was breathed upon the waters as described in *Genesis* in the Bible. Similar descriptions are found through the mystical literature of all spiritual traditions.

Tarot cards having either a spiritual message or similar mystical or alchemical imagery are embodied by the wisdom of Amethyst.

APACHE TEAR

This stone's warning and message of despair, sadness, depression, and negative circumstances may be seen in the Nine of Swords—tears in the night.

Another card, the Three of Swords with its rainy background and three swords piercing a red heart indicate sorrow and heartache. Yet despite negative messages both stone and the Three of Swords card carry a message of hope. While Apache Tear represents the "Dark Night of the Soul" in which one sinks into despair, it also promises that a "Golden Dawn" is coming. The Three of Swords is a heart not only wounded, but one that has been "opened"—albeit suddenly and traumatically—to light and to love. Light, understanding, and love from without pour into the heart and the love hidden within the heart is free to pour forth into the world. Simultaneously sorrows are transformed into acceptance and joy.

AQUAMARINE

When I see this gemstone I think of the King of Swords. For me the message of Aquamarine and the King of Swords speak about the ability to get to the bottom line, use one's intellect and common sense. The suit of Swords speaks of the world of thought, ideas, authority, intellect and rational, left-brained concepts. Aquamarine carries this same message.

GEMSTONE FORECASTING AND OTHER DIVINATION SYSTEMS 129

BLOODSTONE

This stone's message of loving, but troubled relationships may be found in one aspect of the Five of Cups. A cloaked figure concentrates on three spilled cups, yet out of sight (awareness) stand two full cups. All the poor soul can see, however, are the cups tipped on their sides spilling forth their contents. The suit of Cups represents our capacity to feel, intuit, and receive spiritual and instinctive guidance.

Bloodstone and the Five of Cups tell us that we may choose to concentrate attention on hurt feelings and petty misunderstandings or we can turn our attention to the positive aspects of our relationships.

BLUE LACE AGATE

The Tarot's Pages, Knights, and Kings represent well the various aspects of male energy that is the message of this gemstone. While these "royal" cards may represent various aspects and personalities, they also represent issues and conditions. Depending upon what gemstones lie in proximity to Blue Lace Agate, various conditions regarding a "male" will be revealed.

CARNELIAN

Seeking one's muse—apprenticeship or new learning—may be found in the imagery of the Eight of Pentacles if you regard one of the facets of meaning associated with this card as "apprenticeship."

CITRINE

New beginnings and successful cycles may be discovered in one of the interpretations of the Six of Swords—sailing to a new shore. The Two of Wands carries a similar energy in its imagery of charting a new course.

CRAZY LACE AGATE

Movement, change of residence, and relocation is the message of this stone and may be seen also in the Four of Wands. This card speaks of a new home in one of its aspects (also a marriage, a new child, or other positive life passage not indicated by Crazy Lace Agate).

DALMATIAN AGATE

This stone speaks of legal matters and contracts, licenses, regulations, and law. For me the Justice card resonates perfectly.

GEMSTONE FORECASTING AND OTHER DIVINATION SYSTEMS 131

FLUORITE

A well-honed craft, ability, talent, or skill is the message of this stone *and* of the Three of Pentacles. Mystically, the message of the number "three" is one of attained majesty, perfection, and manifestation.

FOSSILIZED DINOSAUR BONE

This gemstone reflects change particularly as it relates to job, career, and profession. There are two Tarot cards that depict people pursuing a craft. The Eight of Pentacles portrays a laborer crafting pentacles with hammer and chisel pursuing his craft. Perhaps he is hoping for a change for the better in his work—a promotion or better pay? In the Two of Cups a man and woman appear to be toasting partnership of some kind—perhaps relating to a business success.

GIRASOL

Girasol represents the sensitive parts of our feelings we don't often share with others except, perhaps, those closest to our hearts, and then only if we have deep trust.

Tarot's Queen of Cups has hidden her feelings and emotions in an elaborate chalice she holds apart from herself. This elaborate, lidded construct shields from view feelings she needs to protect. This is, of course, only one of many interpretations for the Queen of Cups. The Tarot suit of Cups resonates with water, which is associated with feelings and emotions.

When sensitive feelings of hurt, betrayal, and heartache are hidden and unexpressed, the Three of Swords—a wounded heart pierced through by three swords—may also resonate with Girasol.

In the health portion of a reading Girasol is all about drinking adequate amounts of water and having its soothing presence in our environment. It is natural that this gemstone would resonate with the Tarot suit of Cups.

HEMATITE

This gemstone, comprised primarily of iron, has a message for those who hold deep reverence and interest in the past and who preserve the ancient skills and techniques such as blacksmithing, mining, and ironworking. However, the meaning of this card is not limited by metal and ore working but covers all types of ancient crafts. Both the Three of Pentacles and the Eight of Pentacles will be of particular interest to people whose hobbies or careers preserve the tools and handicrafts of antiquity—candle making, spinning, weaving, shoemaking, glassblowing, manual crafts, flint knapping, masonry, and more!

LABRADORITE

This gemstone carries a message of news and sometimes movement or travel by or over water. Tarot cards resonating with this gemstone are the Page of Pentacles and the Knight of Pentacles—both with some type of news to impart. The Knight of Swords may also bring sudden, unexpected news. As to movement over water, the Six of Swords depicts a boatman ferrying a woman and child over a body of water to the opposite shore.

LEPIDOLITE

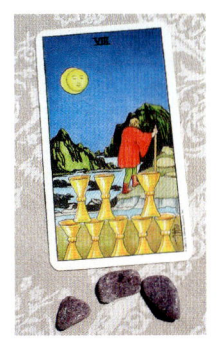

With a message of knowing when to let go, walk away, or release outmoded behaviors and habits, this gemstone resonates well with the Eight of Cups. A person clothed in red walks away from a stack of Cups that no longer serve or hold promise.

LINED AGATE

This stone speaks of our conflicts and hidden fears. Conflicts with others and within us, fear of rejection, fear of the dark, fear of failure, mental confusion and disturbance are all addressed by Lined Agate. The secret hidden by the need to have conflict in one's life is fear. Fears are the demons of our imaginings. The Nine of Swords—tears in the night—denotes dark imaginings, night terrors, and fears arising out of the unknown parts of us. Recognizing a fear as something of our own creation empowers us to overcome it. Conflict embodied in the message of Lined Agate is seen in the Five and Seven of Wands.

MAGNESITE

Karma and fate, and the gift of grace are the messages of this gemstone. Tarot's Wheel of Fortune depicts perfectly this gemstone's message of fate and karma. Three cards suggest the bestowal of Universal Grace. The Ace of Cups depicts the mystical decent of spirit, The Star's image of a goddess pouring fourth water—water is a mystical symbol representing spirit—and The World featuring a woman clothed in royal purple ruling over the elements.

MALACHITE

In readings where I have used both stones and cards, Malachite and the Page of Swords often come up in a session bearing similar messages. "Be on guard." Another card, the Seven of Swords, depicts a sly fellow stealing swords from an encampment. The message here may well be to take steps to protect yourself, your loved ones, or your property. This, too, is Malachite's message.

The Page of Swords stands on a windswept hill holding his sword at ready.

MOONSTONE

Moonstone denotes feminine energy, a girl, a young woman, even a matron, wife or sister. Several Tarot cards reflect feminine energy. Most notably are the Queens of each of the four suits—Pentacles, Swords, Cups, and Wands. For me, The World card illustrates perfectly the "you go girl" energy of Moonstone.

MOSS AGATE

The Empress card of Tarot's major arcana reminds me of the message and energy of Moss Agate—the abundance of Nature, animals, and green, growing things! The concepts of Gaia and Mother Nature bind gemstone and card in my mind.

PINK AVENTURINE

Due to this gemstone's mentor, parental, and wise elder energy, The Hermit card stands out.

PYRITE

This stone's warning of betrayal may be seen in the Ten of Swords depicting someone lying upon the ground, blood pooling from wounds in the back where he/she has been stabbed by ten swords when only one would have been effective. Pyrite warns of an enemy about to be revealed, misconduct, or simply some important detail that has been overlooked.

QUARTZ CRYSTAL

Strength! This facet of meaning is the same as the Strength card in the Tarot's major arcana. A woman subdues a fierce lion with strength of will rather than of body. This is one of the messages of Quartz Crystal. The other message is of positive outcome. More than one Quartz Crystal indicates the movement of energy suggested by the Eight of Wands. When energy moves in this way it is time to put your plans into action!

RED JASPER

Red Jasper's messages of passionate love, for me, resonates with Tarot's The Lover's card

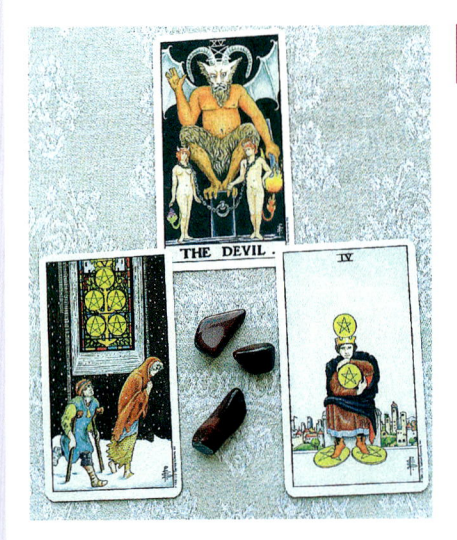

RED TIGER EYE

Ego, and a false belief that perfection may be attained, and intolerance is the message of this gemstone. Red Tiger Eye's message reminds me of Tarot's Devil card—a man and woman stand chained to a horned being that embodies the concepts of limited and false beliefs.

Another card, the Five of Pentacles, suggests extreme poverty. This card bears a message of destitution and sickness of body. It may also indicate poverty of soul. Perfectionists may sacrifice important facets of life—relationships, play, relaxation, and enjoyment—in an unfulfilled quest for perfection. Perfectionists *can* suffer a poverty of spirit if they allow the people and things that make life worth living to dwindle away in an unrelenting quest for perfection.

The Four of Pentacles depicts a wealthy ruler sitting upon a sterile stage. He thinks only of wealth. His love of wealth is such that it fills his heart to the exclusion of all else. It is his foundation and reason for being. He sits with his back to a city where life is being lived in all its variety and abundance. He sits alone and isolated.

RHODOCROSITE

Unconditional love and forgiveness are messages of this gemstone. When we judge others or hold resentment, we place ourselves in bondage to negative emotions. Holding onto negative emotions leads to suffering and mental enslavement. The one at whom anger and resentment are directed is not affected. Forgiveness—relinquishing judgment and resentment—is freeing and makes room for positive energy to enter our lives. Tarot's Eight of Swords illustrates the bondage into which we place ourselves—a prison forged of our own thoughts.

Tarot's Queen of Swords depicts a royal woman who has freed herself by learning to control her thoughts. Her sword is raised in victory. The remains of a severed fetter still encircle one wrist. Perhaps she wears it as a reminder.

RHODONITE

Something unexpected but of a positive nature is promised by this gemstone. Perhaps a gift or surprise of some kind is coming your way! This unexpected boon is not usually monetary although it can be.

The Six of Pentacles depicts two destitute people palms extended receiving golden coins pouring forth from the hand of a well-to-do nobleman. The Seven of Cups is sometimes called the, "Wish Card" and may depict "heart's desires," part of the message of Rhodonite.

ROSE QUARTZ

This stone bears a message of healing and gentle love. For me this message resonates with the Six of Cups. In this image an older child hands a younger one a golden cup filled with flowers. Five other flower-filled cups rest nearby ready to be given. Despite this card's many meanings I see it sending a promise of healing to those who have suffered childhood illness and trauma. I also see an element of healing in the Ace of Pentacles.

SERPENTINE

Serpentine speaks of longtime or priority relationships—a friend, spouse, sibling, or someone with whom we've forged a connection. Four cards, the Two of Cups, Six of Cups, Ten of Cups, and Ten of Pentacles, suggest the various types of relationships found in Serpentine's message.

SNOWFLAKE OBSIDIAN

When I see the Four of Wands I think of this gemstone's message of union (sometimes a marriage) and the balance of opposites. Balance of opposites may be depicted by the Two of Cups—a man and woman who appear as equals. In Snowflake Obsidian's context the union is not necessarily physical as it is with Red Jasper.

SODALITE

Sodalite's message is one of intuition, following your instincts, and honoring your gut feelings and inner wisdom. The Moon in Tarot's major arcana carries a similar meaning. Dreams, meditations, daydreams and flights of fancy often carry messages arising from the deep, secret, and ancient parts of our psyches.

SUNSTONE

Sunshine—both literally and figuratively are indicated by Sunstone. Play and joy are qualities of this card. The Three of Cups—three maids joyfully dancing—remind me of this stone. The Sun of the major arcana also resonates with Sunstone.

TIGER EYE

The Sun card in Tarot bears a message of a "sunny outcome" and things turning out better than anticipated in one layer of its meaning. Tiger Eye, too, speaks of circumstances that have a positive outcome even if appearances are contrary.

TURQUOISE

The Four of Swords portrays the peace and respite that comes upon the heels of turbulence and turmoil. Here is the figure of a knight lying supine upon a tomb or perhaps he is just resting or slumbering in a cool, quiet place. His battle is over. Peace and silence reign. His war swords hang, at rest, points down. One adorns the side of the tomb. A colorful window depicts a peaceful scene. Some may read this card as one of death, which would negate this gemstone/card combination of meaning.

Another fitting card is the Ace of Pentacles. A serene flower and fruit-filled garden waits to bring peace and rest to weary souls at day's end. In this image a spirit hand offers a golden pentacle, symbol of physical abundance and Nature. Peace and abundance infuse this imagery. A message of peace and contentment is also seen in the Nine of Pentacles. Here a noblewoman stands in her garden a falcon upon her wrist. She is robed and surrounded in beauty and appears to be contented and at home in her surroundings.

TURRITELLA AGATE

This gemstone suggests an increase in money through some avenue such as a pay raise, an inheritance, a bonus, or some other avenue of plenty. The Six of Pentacles show two souls receiving coins. The Ten of Cups may be celebrating increased monetary abundance—the symbolic attaining of the gold at the end of the rainbow.

UNAKITE

The Five of Pentacles echoes Unakite's message of stress, pain, and illness. In this card two souls dressed in rags, one limping, endure a night's freezing blizzard while a chapel window glows warmly behind them unnoticed.

Unakite's message of burning one's energy-candle at both ends is reflected by the Two of Pentacles. In this image a jester juggles two pentacles in an eternal motion while trying to balance on one foot. A turbulent, storm-tossed sea is featured behind him. The messages of both card and crystal denote turmoil, trying to do too much, and misapplication of energy in too many directions.

YELLOW QUARTZ

The warm, yellow color of this gemstone reminds me of golden light issuing from a cozy home's windows. A love of home reminds me of the Ten of Pentacles with its depiction of a happy, abundant home and family. Hearth and home and the "ground" of one's being are messages of Yellow Quartz. Hearth is *earth* with an *H*. Hearth is our particular place upon the earth we call "home." Here, at our home hearth we have our life and sanctuary.

As you study the messages of crystals and gemstones you will find there is harmonious resonance between their messages and those of your favorite divination method.

CHAPTER 7

Acquiring, Energizing, and Caring For Crystals and Gemstones

THERE ARE AVENUES FOR ACQUIRING THE CRYSTALS AND GEMSTONES needed for the divination collection. The easiest way to obtain what you need is to purchase them from a variety of sources that sell crystals and gemstones. This will be the route most people will take. Further on in this chapter there are suggestions on the types of shops and markets where crystals and gemstones may be purchased.

Then there is the hard way—not hard, really, but more time consuming, a lot of fun, and a great adventure—collecting them yourself straight from Nature!

If you are interested in collecting your own gemstones and crystals from natural habitats, there are guidebooks for many states featuring known collecting sites, including my book, *Rockhounding California,* and the *Gem Trails of (State name)* series of books which includes most of the western states as well as Pennsylvania and New Jersey. These books list collecting sites with maps, mileages, and road conditions for each state. Hobbyists who collect their own rocks, minerals, and gemstones call themselves "rockhounds."

> I collected many of my divination stones from areas where I prospected for gold and minerals. I brought them home and cleaned, shaped, and polished them. During this process I experienced their messages for humankind and their evolutionary purposes.

Using these books as a guide you can find some of the crystals and gemstones used in gemstone divination. Please check the website of the publisher of this book, Gem Guides Book Co. at *www.gemguidesbooks.com* for titles and availability.

CRYSTAL AND GEMSTONE DIVINATION

If you decide to collect your own crystals and gemstones, most will need to be cleaned, cut and polished with rock-cutting (lapidary) equipment, or broken up, and tumble-polished. Rose Quartz, and especially Quartz Crystal may be used in their natural state but may require removal of oxide stains and a good scrubbing to remove dirt from nooks and crannies.

There will be costs involved in purchasing rock cutting and polishing machines—lapidary equipment. Prices are more reasonable when purchasing used equipment. Check the local classifieds or eBay® for lapidary equipment and supplies. Contacting local gem and mineral clubs is another resource for finding used lapidary equipment and tumble polishers. Many local and junior colleges offer evening lapidary courses and have equipment available free for registered students and may rent use of the equipment for onsite use for a nominal fee.

How-to books are available on the simple process of tumble-polishing stones at rock shops and online. Check local libraries, as well.

All crystals and gemstones used in the divination collection, or listed as substitutes, are abundant and commonly found in shops and online. If finding and polishing your own gemstones sounds like too great an investment in time and expense, purchasing all the stones and crystals for your divination collection is the simplest and most economic means for most people.

Even if you decide to prospect for your own divination stones there will still be some you will need to purchase. Not all the gemstones used for divination come from North America. Some are imported from overseas and have messages important to humankind.

Following are sources where you will find, ready at hand, all the crystals and gemstones—or their substitutes—needed to complete your divination collection.

Initially, when writing this book I planned to list names and addresses of sources for purchasing crystals and gemstones. However, I found that favorite sources of mine have gone out of business, downsized, or changed the focus of their business to jewelry. Some have gone from retail sales to wholesale marketing only. Internet and hobby magazine searches turned up new names and sources. While I could list these companies, I feel that due to the ever-changing market such specific information would

ACQUIRING, ENERGIZING, CARING FOR CRYSTALS, GEMSTONES

quickly become obsolete. Also, it would omit new sources that arise after publication of this book. Therefore, I will list the types of sources and shops to visit and specific words to look for in the yellow pages and input into your computer search engine. In this way you will have the most up-to-date information without wasting time with sources that can't provide what you need.

NEW AGE SHOPS

Here the selection is very good and you will find many, if not all, of the crystals and gemstones you are looking for. New Age shops carry books on all aspects of using crystals and gemstones for meditation and healing if you are interested in discovering more about other fascinating facets of mineral wisdom.

ROCK SHOPS

Most towns and cities have rock shops featuring both tumble polished and natural gemstones. Rock shops often carry huge selections of sparkling natural crystals and tumble-polished gemstones ready to be made into jewelry or added to your divination collection. Rock shop prices are reasonable as well. Look for rock shops in your local telephone book under "mineral shops," "rock shops," "gems and minerals" and "lapidary."

Be aware that what are marketed as "mineral specimens" will be more costly as they are representative of what collectors deem as "mineral perfection" based on crystal formation, color, size, or locale; also, mineral specimens may be too fragile for use in the divination collection.

GEM AND MINERAL SHOWS

Check your local classifieds to see when your community is hosting a gem and mineral show. Numerous vendors displaying and selling beautiful collectible and commonly found crystals and gemstones from around the world attend these shows. Some of the larger shows feature a hundred or more vendors!

There is always a large selection of crystals and gemstones available and prices are competitive and reasonable. All the crystals and gemstones used in the divination collection are considered "semi-precious" which means they are commonly available *and* reasonably priced. At mineral shows you will find other wonderful gem and mineral treasures as well.

146   CRYSTAL AND GEMSTONE DIVINATION

Mineral shows are a great place to find a vast variety of crystals and gemstones for your divination collection. Prices are reasonable and competitive.

In addition to finding crystals and gemstones for your divination collection, there are many other gemstone treasures to be found.

ON-LINE

The world of online shopping is growing by leaps and bounds. eBay® is just one source of many online crystal and gemstone sources. In your search engine simply type the name of the crystal or gemstone you are looking for and you will be presented with dozens of sources and choices.

OTHER SOURCES

Many museums have natural history displays featuring gems and minerals of the world and sell tumble polished gemstones and small crystals in their gift shops. Renaissance fairs and sidewalk art fairs are places where gemstone vendors display and sell gemstone jewelry and loose gemstones.

Don't overlook bead shops and jewelry supply stores! Many of the gemstones used in the divination collection may be purchased in the form of beads. Just be sure that the beads are large enough to be easily handled and seen. Jewelry supply stores will sell "findings," or metal settings, for those who make their own jewelry as well as stocking tumble polished gemstones and crystal points.

Care and Cleansing of Crystals and Gemstones

Now that you have acquired crystals and gemstones it is time to cleanse them. It is important to cleanse your stones soon after purchase before you use them. Even if you have found, cut and polished them yourself, you will still need to clean your stones prior to using them for any metaphysical or healing purposes, including divination.

As a rule, any crystals and gemstones purchased for wearing as amulets or jewelry should also be cleansed to remove any negative imprinting or grime from handling they may be carrying.

The processes of mining, transporting, cutting, polishing, and shipping your crystals and stones imbues them with all types of energy and imprinting. After mining and shipping, cutting, polishing, and handling your gemstones will probably be sorted, displayed, and shipped again. They will have been handled many times by numerous people with diverse concerns, problems, thoughts, energies, etc. Your stones arrive with an array of transient imprinting (along with fingerprints and perspiration) from all these experiences.

To return newly purchased crystals and gemstones to their pure, energetic state for use in meditation, dreamwork, healing, or divination they must be cleansed of all these extraneous, chaotic energies. Cleansing your crystals and gemstones returns them to a condition that allows you to more easily tap into their mineral wisdom and healing capabilities.

THE SALT AND SUN CLEANSE

One of the best and most popular ways to cleanse your gemstones is to soak them in saltwater.

Saltwater Cleanse
One pint, cool water
One handful salt, approximately ¼-cup

Pour a pint of cool water (spring, purified, tap, or distilled) into bowl. It doesn't matter of what material the bowl is made. Gently add your gemstones rather than dropping them into the bowl. Add the salt over the top of the stones. You can use either table or sea salt, although sea salt or any unadulterated or kosher salt is preferred. Most table salt has added fillers and de-clumping agents. These additives won't harm your crystals but won't add anything beneficial either. Allow the stones to soak in the salted water for several hours or overnight.

You will need water, salt, and a towel for the stones to dry on. Letting the stones dry in a sunny spot outside will re-energize them.

You may notice that the soaking water gradually becomes murky or cloudy. Some of this may be due to trace minerals natural to sea salt. The

ACQUIRING, ENERGIZING, CARING FOR CRYSTALS, GEMSTONES 149

saltwater soak has also pulled dust, grime, and grease from handling, as well as negative and mixed energy imprinting from the stones.

Gently pour the saltwater and gemstones into a colander. Run cool water over the stones until they are rinsed completely. Remove them from the colander and place them evenly—not touching—on a clean cotton towel to air dry. If weather permits, I like to air dry my stones on a towel in a sunny spot on the stone bench in my garden.

Exposure to sunlight after cleansing re-energizes your stones. In the winter a table or shelf in a sunny window works fine.

Leave your gemstones and crystals in the sun for only an hour or so. Some gemstones and crystals are artificially colored. Amethyst and citrine are two types that are commonly "color enhanced." Continual long-term exposure to sunlight may eventually fade color.

The soaking water may turn cloudy due to grime and negative energy on the stones. Or, it may be due to the type of salt used.

I like to air dry my divination gemstones in a sunny spot in my garden.

Artificially coloring gemstones is a common way to deepen hue for the jewelry and gemstone markets. Dying or heating are the two most popular methods of enhancing color. These processes do not harm the stones from an energetic standpoint; however, there is usually no way to tell if stones you are purchasing have been color enhanced unless a vendor chooses to disclose this information.

The saltwater and sunshine cleanse is one of the best treatments for newly acquired stones. I cleanse my divination crystals and gemstones once a month in this manner. My household crystals are cleansed twice a year under normal conditions. After illness or negative occurrences, such as an argument, I cleanse them as soon as possible.

Stones used for healing or chakra balancing should be cleansed after each use. Those used in dreamwork or meditation may be cleansed once a month or so. When using or wearing gemstones to attract conditions such as love, peace, prosperity, courage, etc. they should be cleansed after their task has been accomplished.

SALT AND MUGWORT CHARGE AND CLEANSE

Crystals and gemstones, especially those used for divination purposes benefit from a saltwater and mugwort soak followed by a Moonlight bath.

Saltwater and Mugwort Soak
1 cup, cool water
1 cup cooled, strained mugwort tea
¼-cup salt

The Moon and mugwort soak will enhance the psychic connection with your divination stones.

Place your gemstones in a bowl. Pour in one cup of cool water. Add cooled mugwort tea (one tablespoon of dried mugwort leaf steeped in one cup boiling water until cool, then strained) and sprinkle on the salt. Let your stones soak for at least at least two or more hours.

The herb mugwort has long been used to cleanse divination tools such as mirrors and crystal balls. Mugwort leaf may be found at most health food stores where it is sold

ACQUIRING, ENERGIZING, CARING FOR CRYSTALS, GEMSTONES 151

as a digestive-aid. Or, you may order it from my website, *www.gailsgardenofgems.com*. Mugwort listed on my website is organically grown in my gardens, hand harvested, and dried at my home, Heartsease Cottage. Therefore, availability may vary depending upon weather and the production of the plants themselves.

A moonlight/mugwort soak is best done one, two, or three days before a full moon. The evening after your salt and mugwort soak set your crystals and gemstones on a clean cotton towel in a spot, indoors or out, where they will soak up the moonlight. After resting in moonlight for several hours your divination collection will be charged with both mystery and moonlight! And, your stones will be magnetized to stimulate the intuitive and psychic parts of your nature and that of your clients.

If you give crystal and gemstone readings to others on a regular basis, treat your divination collection to a monthly salt and mugwort cleanse and moonlight bath. This combination deep cleans your stones of accumulated energies absorbed from a variety of people and recharges them for the psychic work of divination.

Crystals and gemstones get tired! They are easily imprinted through handling and exposure to varied thoughts and emotions. Its time to cleanse your stones when their energy feels less crisp, or when communication with them seems muddled or fuzzy, and they appear or "feel" dull in color, energy, or luster. When they reach this state it's actually past the time to cleanse them. If you get in the habit of cleaning your divination collection regularly, before they become jammed with a jumble of energies, you will keep the lines of communication between yourself and the mineral realm crisp and clear. How often to cleanse your gemstones will, of course, depend upon how often and for what you use them for. A good general rule is to perform a saltwater and/or moonlight and mugwort cleanse at least once a month. If you give readings to others occasionally or on a regular basis you'll want to cleanse them more often.

You will find the following quick-cleanse methods helpful because it isn't always practical to cleanse them by soaking between client readings.

SMOKE CLEANSE

1 stick of pure, natural incense or one teaspoon of loose dried herbs or sage, cedar, lavender, or juniper bundle

The smoke of herbs and incense may be used to give divination stones a quick cleanse between clients.

Loose herbs are a little more trouble to use because they must be burned on charcoal disks used specifically for this purpose. Charcoal disks for burning loose, dry herbs are available at New Age shops and stores specializing in incense and magic. While the tablets are easy to use, a tablet requires ten to twenty minutes to fully ignite before herbs may be added.

Loose, dry herbs of mugwort, sage (white or garden types), hyssop, rosemary, lavender, juniper, cedar, or the resins of myrrh, copal, or frankincense may be used. All of these herbs and resins are known for their purifying and cleansing qualities.

Mugwort, garden sage (used in poultry stuffing), rosemary, hyssop, and lavender were used in Europe and the New World for their purification properties. Hyssop was used to cleanse and purify the altars and atmosphere of Greek Temples.

Juniper is a classic Asian purification herb, especially in Mongolia and Tibet while white sage and copal are used in the Americas. Frankincense has a long and honored history and tradition of use in the Middle East to purify and sweeten the air. As your chosen herbs or resins smolder, fan the smoke toward and over your tray of gemstones. Allow the scentless charcoal tablet to burn out or remove the bowl to another room before your next client arrives. Adding clean sand or kitty litter insulates the bowl and keeps it from getting too hot. Fill the bowl about half full and place the charcoal tablet on top. Use a match to light the tablet. Saltpeter in the charcoal

Be cautious as the smoldering charcoal tablet gets quite hot and may overheat the bowl.

ACQUIRING, ENERGIZING, CARING FOR CRYSTALS, GEMSTONES   153

allows it to ignite. Your tablet will "sparkle" and pop a little as the saltpeter ignites. It takes ten to twenty minutes before the charcoal is glowing sufficiently to smolder dry herbs. When gray ash covers half the tablet you may begin sprinkling on dry herbs. I use this method when I have twenty or more minutes to wait for the charcoal to ready itself for the herbs.

Easiest and fastest for a quick smoke cleanse are incense sticks, cones, and smudging bundles of dried herbs. Many commercial incense sticks and cones are made from "fragrance" oils that are synthetic and are of no value for cleansing your stones.

> If you choose incense be sure to use only that which is made from real plant or spice essences impregnated into charcoal.

I recommend Auroshikha and the Bombay Incense Company for stick incense, or any other companies that make theirs from real plants and essential oils. See *sources* for purchasing information on Auroshikha and Bombay Incense Company. Auroshikha incense is sometimes available on eBay®.

Frankincense, lavender, sage, rosemary, and cedar are aromas to look for in incense sticks. These herbs and resins have long been used for their ability to cleanse the atmosphere of sites, buildings, and objects by raising vibrations and eliminating heavy and unclean energies.

To use stick incense hold the "stick" end or insert it into an incense burner. Light the other end then blow out the flame so that it glows and begins to smolder. Pass the smoldering incense back and forth over your bowl or tray of divination stones for several seconds. Or you may fan the incense smoke toward your gemstones with your hand or a large feather.

Extinguish the unused portion of the incense stick by placing the smoldering end into sand or stubbing it out on the edge of the incense holder. Or, you may allow the stick to smolder and perfume the atmosphere of the room to clear residual energies between clients.

Keep in mind that not all people enjoy the scent of incense. Some with asthma, hay fever, or respiratory problems may even have adverse reactions to it. You may wish to adjourn briefly to another room to cleanse your gemstones between readings if you expect to have sensitive clients arriving soon.

Herb bundles used for smudging such as those used by Native Americans are another choice. These usually come in the following single herb or herb combinations of white sage, lavender, or cedar. While I associate the smell of smoldering white sage with cleansing and purification, others find the scent reminiscent of stale sweat. If you use white sage or a combination of sage and lavender or cedar, you may want to do a brief "between clients" smudge of your divination stones outdoors. Simply light one end of the herb bundle and blow out the flames to get the smoldering started. Place the smoldering end of the bundle into a pottery bowl or abalone shell.

Herb bundles tend to shed bits of smoldering herb and ash that could damage furniture or carpets. Also, you won't want bits of smoldering herb falling onto your divination stones. Pass bowl and bundle over your herbs, back and forth, for several seconds fanning the smoke over the gemstones. Extinguish the smoldering end of the herb bundle in a bowl of sand. Leave the bundle in the sand to be sure it is completely extinguished. It may be left there for re-lighting and reuse at a future time.

Incense sticks and smudging bundles are fast ways to cleanse your stones between readings, healing sessions, or chakra balancing. You will still need to use a saltwater cleanse periodically, once a week or monthly depending upon the frequency of use your gemstones undergo.

Energizing of Crystals and Gemstones

ELEMENTAL ENERGIZING

In their natural outdoor habitats crystals and gemstones are exposed to wind, rain, and sun and are energized by this contact. To keep the energy of your stones at a high level it helps to energize them with wind, rain, and sun especially if they see a lot of use.

Energizing your crystals and gemstones by exposure to the elements accomplishes for them what a great vacation does for you! While a good soak and scrub in the tub

ACQUIRING, ENERGIZING, CARING FOR CRYSTALS, GEMSTONES 155

cleans both your body and "fluffs" your aura, a good getaway-vacation re-energizes and revives on all levels.

Time spent in the Sun and Moonlight has already been discussed to some degree. Sunlight and Moonlight are great energizers after saltwater cleansing. Sunlight revitalizes stones in a positive manner after frequent long-term usage for divination or healing. Sunlight also aids in priming them for transforming the atmosphere of a room particularly after arguments or if a room's energy seems lifeless or flat.

Exposure to rain will vivify a divination set, as well. A light, cleansing rain or exposure to moderate rainfall accompanied by thunder and lightening energizes rocks, minerals, crystals, and gemstones of all types.

Energize stones in Sunlight for wearing or carrying to attract desired conditions and for healing and chakra balancing. Moonlight renews gemstones' psychic-magnetic qualities for mineral realm communication, divination, dreamwork and meditation.

In their natural environments surface minerals and stones are stimulated by the negative ions that accompany rain showers and thunderstorms.

If you choose to energize your stones by exposure to thunderstorms be especially careful of exposing yourself to lightening strikes! While chances are of being struck by lightening are only one in 700,000, approximately 73 people are killed each in the United States alone, and about 300 more are injured by lightning strikes.

Avoid putting your stones out in torrential downpours as they could get washed away. To energize crystals by rainfall place them on a glass or plastic tray in a single layer. Leave them out for about an hour. Bring them in to air dry on a clean cotton towel before use.

Simply rinsing crystals under cool running water is also a good interim method of re-energizing and cleaning them between saltwater cleanses. Be sure they are completely dry before giving a reading.

QUARTZ CRYSTAL CLUSTER ENERGIZING

Another favorite method of clearing your divination collection of accumulated psychic detritus is by using a large quartz crystal cluster. Crystal clusters have the benefit of being able to cleanse other stones. Clusters don't need frequent cleansing either. I still give my household clusters a twice yearly cleansing and use them in the interim to energize my divination collection and crystal and gemstone jewelry.

To use a large crystal cluster to revivify your crystals and gemstones, clear a spot in the center of your divination tray large enough to place the cluster. Scoot your divination stones all around the edge of the cluster. Some of your stones should be in direct contact with the cluster. Others will not be. Be sure all your divination stones are touching one another and that some are in contact with the cluster. Vibrational resonance between the stones and those in contact with the cluster will revitalize all of the gemstones in the tray. Leave this arrangement in place for several hours or overnight.

Another energizing method is to place a large quartz crystal cluster in a bowl of water deep enough that the cluster is completely submerged. Gently pour your divination gemstones into the bowl and over the cluster. Add a handful of salt. The salt cleanses the gemstones and the cluster helps to energize them. This is a good method to use if you cannot expose your gemstones to Sun- or Moonlight. Leave the stones and cluster to soak for several hours or overnight. Carefully rinse the gemstones and crystal cluster in cool water and allow to air dry on a soft, clean towel.

Drape crystal and gemstone amulets on a quartz crystal cluster overnight to revitalize their energy. Gemstone rings, bracelets, and earrings may also be laid over crystal clusters, as well.

Crystals and gemstones are energized by contact with large quartz crystal clusters. Jewelry may also be energized by contact with a crystal cluster.

Gemstone jewelry that is worn continually, as well as crystals and stones used frequently for healing and metaphysical work need cleansing and reviving from time to time. Continual use and exposure to various auras, events, and emotions tends to congest crystals and gemstones. It is important to keep their energy fresh, clean, and vital!

Storing Your Crystals and Gemstones

There are likely to be periods of time when you don't use your crystals and gemstones, especially if you only do occasional readings for yourself or others. The best place to store your gemstones is in their tray on a shelf, table, or fireplace mantle. Try not to keep them in closed cupboards or in drawers for long periods. Storing them in the dark, away from light and air circulation will diminish their inherent energy.

Gemstones and crystals in natural cavities and vugs deep within the ground are kept vital and energized by Earth's magnetic currents and exposure to surrounding minerals, igneous processes, and seismic movement. Drawers and cupboards provide no useful stimulation other than movement as they are opened and closed.

If you store your stones in the open—up high where small children and pets won't spill or scatter them—they will energize and cleanse the atmosphere of whatever room they occupy. An occasional saltwater cleanse and Sun- or Moonlight energizing will dispel dust, and any musty and negative energy your stones absorb over time that occurs from surrounding energies.

Keeping your crystals clean and energized will keep them at their best for energizing the energy in your home.

Avoid storing your crystals and gemstones in sunny south, west, or east windows for long periods. They may fade due to sun exposure. Long-term sun exposure fades stones in their natural environments and on your windowsill! Dyed and artificially colored stones are even more likely to fade with long-term exposure. A couple hours of sun exposure is beneficial to your crystals and gemstones. Long-term sun exposure is unlikely to ruin their energy. However, faded gemstones have diminished visual appeal to the querist.

A cloth bag will keep your divination stones together and safe from loss when you travel.

If you take your divination stones on trips as I occasionally do you will want to carry them in a fabric bag so they don't get lost. Taking them with you when you travel insures they are available for self-readings or for giving readings to others. Also, your crystals and gemstones are a quick and reliable way to energize the atmosphere of any hotel rooms you may be occupying during your travels. Do not, however, leave your gemstones in view when you leave your room for the day. While most hotel employees are honest and won't trifle with guests' belongings, a tray of colorful crystals and gemstones may prove too attractive to resist! And you may find that one or more stones turn up missing next time you give a reading.

When you leave your hotel room, place your stones in their carrying bag and take them with you or lock them in your car. Carried in a purse or travel pouch they will protect and energize your travel by foot, automobile, train, bus, or plane.

A suggestion for airplane travel is to keep your gemstones in your carryon bag when you fly. You can pack their tray and pad in your suitcase but the crystals and gemstones should go with you!

Nighttime in your hotel room is when you may place your gemstones out in their tray to energize the atmosphere while you relax and sleep. When you shower or bathe, place them on the counter in the bathroom so they will affect the bathroom atmosphere and the water in which you are bathing in a positive manner.

In the next chapter you will find many other interesting and wonderful uses for your crystals and gemstones besides divination!

CHAPTER 8

Other Uses for Your Crystals and Gemstones

IN THIS CHAPTER WE WILL EXAMINE other uses for your divination crystals and gemstones besides foretelling. I'll also share *methods* for using the stones to create circumstances and conditions

Meditation and Visualization with Your Divination Stones

The method for meditating or visualizing with stones from your divination collection is fun and easy. First select one or more of one type of crystal or gemstone that best fit the purpose and goal of your meditation and visualization. Referring to Chapter 2—*The Hidden Messages in Crystals and Gemstone*s will help you pick the stones whose energies are best aligned with your particular goal**.** Or use one of the great New Age crystal and gemstone guides on the market to aid in the selection of your stones.

For general meditation purposes Amethyst, Rose Quartz, or Clear Quartz Crystal are commonly used. Jasper of all types is useful when attempting to project the consciousness or for any type of shamanistic work.

For instance, if I want to meditate with the purpose of visualizing an increase in prosperity I might select one or more of the Turritella Agates from the divination basket. Citrine is a wonderful choice for visualizing new opportunities. Meditate with Aquamarine to help you formulate your business plans. Meditating with Fossilized Dinosaur Bone may help you get that job promotion you've been working toward!

Once you have decided on the type of crystal or gemstone best suited to your purpose you may want to select all three of that type. Three is a number that symbolizes manifestation and is based upon the ancient Law of the Triangle wherein two conditions combine to create a third.

Specifically, the Law of the Triangle relates to the manifestation of matter or conditions. The universal force of attraction is inherent in spirit energy. A pattern imprinted upon spirit energy engages the force of attraction or magnetism. Electrons of matter (the densest form of spirit energy) respond to that attraction by drawing negative and positive polarities of other particles to themselves in accordance with the imprinted pattern. This results in either a manifested condition or the creation of matter in the form of objects or things.

Spirit energy is all around us. It is fertile and fruitful. It is what fills the spaces that exist between molecules of matter. It is imprintable and malleable. It is organized via thought-energy.

Many crystals form as a result of the Law of the Triangle.

Four types of gemstones in the divination set illustrate the Law of the Triangle. These four are carbonates having triangular ions (CO_3): Rhodocrosite, Magnesite, Turqurenite, and Malachite. These four gemstones are useful for manifestation work.

Molecules of elements occurring within mineral rich precipitate attract and repel one another according to polarity and vibratory frequency. From this process arise crystals of all types and shapes—cubic, hexagonal, rhombic.

Using the stones from your divination set you can enhance your visualization successes by entraining the wisdom and application of the Law inherent within them. You don't have to understand the chemistry or metaphysics behind the Law; you only have to be open and receptive to the action of the Law within the stones that you are using.

Retire to your meditation area. Lighting a candle and some incense help to create the proper psychic atmosphere and mood for your meditation. Music of a restful, meditative type—or rhythmic drumming—helps further set the stage for meditation. Sitting or lying comfortably on the floor, a chair, mat or bed will help the body and alpha mind to relax its demands upon your attention.

Now hold your stones in your hand (whichever hand seems most right and natural to you) and close your eyes. Visualize the stone or stones you are holding and the purpose or goal for which you selected them. If desired you may silently repeat a word or short phrase as a mantra that describes the purpose or goal of your meditation, "increased prosperity," "finding my soul mate," "sending healing to (name of individual)," "finding my right work," and so on. As you repeat the mantra-phrase visualize the outcome you desire. Leave the details to the Universe. Another caveat is that you *must* as much as possible eliminate any beliefs, fears, limitations, or conditioning associated with the manifestation of your desire! Disbelief in your ability to manipulate spirit energy, doubt that the mineral realm can assist you, belief that you are unworthy to receive, fear that you are not worthy, or a conviction that you cannot create your own reality can thwart your efforts. While we cannot completely expunge this type of mental conditioning from our minds, we can *suspend* limited conditioning and beliefs by excluding them as thought forms from our visualization. If they pop up, dismiss them and return to your visualization.

> Do not visualize how you want your goal to manifest, or whom you may desire a relationship with. Merely, visualize the end result or condition you want to manifest.

After visualizing your desired condition for several minutes, now *imagine* that you do indeed have that which you've visualized. Use each of your senses. *See* yourself enjoying the condition and sharing its benefits with others. *Feel* what it is like to live your desired condition and circumstance. *Taste* the celebratory champagne with which you will rejoice over the arrival of your desire. *Hear* the sounds that may accompany your desired condition. *Smell* any aromas or scents associated with your desired condition— the scent of a lover's hair or skin, the smell of newly minted currency, etc. Use every sense—imagination, touch, sight, hearing, smell, taste—to experience as much as possible how it *feels* to have achieved your goal. Then thank the Universal powers for this wonderful gift of your desire fulfilled!

Even though your desire has not yet manifested in present time, the mere act of expressing gratitude creates the conditions needed for your desire to begin to come true for you. All things are created in thought and spirit before condensing into the physical world! Your visualization begins this process. Thoughts first. Things second!

In the quantum field all things exist simultaneously. There is no past, present, and future as we conceive it with our limited perceptions. Our brains cannot take in the entirety of the concept of simultaneous existence; therefore, our consciousness breaks time into manageable segments that we call past, present, and future. In the quantum world you already have what you desire! Visualization prepares you to *realize* what already exists within your sphere but are *unaware* of as yet. We cannot see something unless we have a *realization* of the *experience* of it! An example of this was given by some early Anglo explorers when they encountered a primitive tribe isolated from other cultures because they lived on a remote island. The explorers cited that the tribe members could not *see* the ships anchored in the bay because they had no concept of floating craft in any form. It was not until the explorers were able to bring the concept into the *realization* of the inhabitants that they were able to *see* the ships floating offshore. I'm not sure I believe this tale but it does illustrate the point I am describing regarding visualization and the power to manifest desires!

> The only void between you and your fulfilled desire is the realization of its existence. You cannot know a thing or enounter it as part of your reality until it is realized as part of your experience.

While you are meditating and visualizing you may become aware that the stones in your hand are warming, cooling, or tingling. Be only mildly aware of this, then shift your thoughts back to your visualization. The action of the stones in your hand is your signal that you and they are sharing a process.

When your visualization session is finished allow your consciousness to return to everyday awareness. Go about your life with the *knowledge* and *confidence* that your desire is in the process of manifesting into physical reality. Do some small thing each day toward your goal. It needn't be a big thing...a bit of research, reading, making a list...something. This helps ground your dream or desire into reality sooner.

You may wish to wear the three stones you used in your meditation in a pouch as an amulet for several days. Wearing or carrying these particular stones that have aided you in creating a desired pattern within the spiritual realm will further aid in magnetizing your desired condition to you. They will continue to vibrate in accordance with your visualization on your behalf. Over a period of several days use this method to meditate and visualize the condition or thing you wish to manifest into your life.

Repeat the process occasionally each week to keep the energy active until you achieve your desire. Revisiting this process over a period of time sets the pattern of your desire in the realms of creativity and makes it a "Law unto Self."

> Each time you perform your visualization, consign its fulfillment to the Universal powers by releasing any doubt and negative emotional attachment to the outcome that may be part of your conditioning or belief system. This is a very important step.

Writing and drawing your desire are additional techniques for giving your desire present-time, physical reality. A fun method for aiding in bringing your desire into present-time reality is called "treasure mapping." You will need a piece of poster board or poster paper from a stationary or craft store. Match the color of poster paper to your desire. The following color list will aid you in matching poster color to the cosmic vibration that will aid in accomplishing your desire.

1. Red—will power, passion, life force, strength, healing of inflammation, sexuality.
2. Pink—love, healing, de-stressing, calming, self-love, happiness, innocence.
3. Orange—sensuality, attraction, personal power, self-worth, luck, and success.
4. Yellow—change, movement and travel, alertness, communication, imagination, and creativity.
5. Green—growth, fertility, healing, gardening, money, luck, grounding and balancing.
6. Blue—sleep, meditation, dreams, peace, cooling, calming, purifying, reduction of pain.

7. Purple—spirituality, mysticism, meditation, healing, peace, calming, antidepressive, angelic realms.
8. White—psychism, purity, luck, protection, substitutes for all colors, angelic and devic realms.
9. Black—protection, absorbs negativity, accesses the subconscious, mystery, night, dreams, and inner work.
10. Gray—elder work, grounding, calming, mentors, parents, and twilight.

On your poster paper write a brief sentence or your meditation mantra that describes your desire. Use colored pens or paints, if you want. Glue or tape up images or symbols that depict your desire. Search magazines and newspapers for appropriate pictures and symbols. Cut out descriptive words and phrases and tape these onto your poster board. Decorate your board in an attractive and symbolic manner that depicts your desired result. Use glitter! Anything that stimulates your imaginative and creative powers! Now hang your treasure map in a spot where you will see it daily.

Let's recap the meditation/visualization process.

1. Select the crystals or gemstones appropriate to your desire.
2. Set the mood – a quiet place, incense, candles, and music or soft drumming.
3. Relax.
4. Visualize the stones you are holding and their metaphysical purpose.
5. Repeat a short phrase or mantra describing your desire.
6. Use your senses to imagine, see, feel, hear, taste, and smell conditions associated with your desire.
7. Thank the Universe for the fulfillment of your desire.
8. Arise from your meditation confidant that your desire is manifesting.
9. Release negative or limiting belief systems that will confuse the pattern you are imprinting upon the spirit realm.
10. Wear or carry the stones used in your meditation/visualization to aid in magnetizing your desire into your life.
11. Repeat this process occasionally to make your desire "a Law unto Self."
12. Write or draw your desired condition or make a treasure map to further aid in magnetizing your desire into physical reality.

Crystal and Gemstone Dreamwork

Dreamwork is a method used for working with your subconscious. Paying attention to your dreams will enable you to become more aware of what your intuition, emotions, and body may be signaling you.

Dreamwork is useful for revealing fears, limitations, desires, and conveying warnings. Becoming aware of these messages from within allows us to live more consciously and with greater awareness. We learn to know ourselves. We discover our strengths so that we may work with them. Similarly, we also discover our limitations so that we may conquer or dispel them.

Dreams may even reveal the seeds of illness that haven't yet manifested in our bodies or into everyday awareness. Cancers and other illnesses sometimes reveal themselves through dreams but we are not taught to pay attention to these messages arising from within. In our culture we are not taught to listen with the subtle senses that communicate through dreams, daydreams, and intuition. We can, however, retrain ourselves to pick up these faint messages arising from within.

Crystals and gemstones aid in identifying subtle inner messages, and help in developing lucid dreaming—the ability to remember dreams and to interact within them in a conscious manner.

We do not need to be helpless victims trapped in our own dreamscapes! We can learn to direct and move consciously within our dreams.

I used to have a recurring childhood nightmare in which a huge bee was after me. I remember waking up terrified and gasping for air. The dream occurred for years until one time my fear became anger and I turned and faced the menacing bee. It simply dwindled in size until it vanished. I never had the dream again. My bee dream was a metaphor for facing my fears. A fear may loom large in the mind. Yet when faced it may actually hold little substance. Simultaneously my fear of real bees dwindled and today I can work in the garden next to the flowers they are buzzing around without any adverse reaction.

For dreamwork select crystals or gemstones that will be helpful such as Amethyst, Sodalite, etc. New Age crystal and gemstone guides can help you select appropriate crystals. After selecting your gemstones meditate with them prior to retiring for the

CRYSTAL AND GEMSTONE DIVINATION

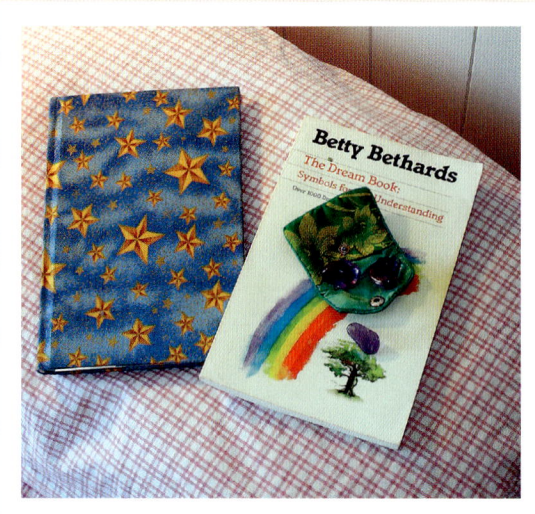

For dreamwork you'll need a journal to record your dreams, a dream interpretation guide, your chosen crystals and a small bag to hold them so they don't get lost.

night. Visualize what you would like to accomplish in the way of remembering and directing your dreams. Place the stones into a soft pouch and insert this under your pillow. As you drift into sleep gently hold in mind that which you wish to work on. Hold the thought that you will be taking an active role in determining the outcome of your dreams. Pay attention to your dreams and record them in a journal upon waking. If you have a recurring dream, create an imaginary dialogue with the characters of your dream before falling asleep. Tell them what you want to accomplish and ask for their help.

It may take several sessions before you notice any change in the way you dream. Don't give up. It can take time to imprint upon the subconscious what you are trying to do and to change existing dream patterns.

Many dreams are "processing" dreams in which our minds process and file mundane activities and sensations encountered during waking hours. Be sure to jot down your impressions upon awaking because dreams fade quickly.

Important dreams with meaningful messages may be in color, more vivid in detail, or particularly easy to recall upon waking.

Don't forget that napping is a potent vehicle for engaging the subconscious mind. My most important dreams occur in the early morning hours and during naps (when I take the time to nap)! Discover when and under what conditions your own dreams are most likely to speak powerfully to you.

The subconscious mind speaks to us using symbols. While dreams may convey concrete messages, they generally communicate to us through symbols. While we may understand the meaning behind many symbols occurring in dreams, some are too obscure. A dream interpretation guide is an important adjunct to recognizing what your inner self may be trying to relate through its use of symbols. Dream guides may be purchased from most bookstores and New Age shops. Rely first on your own feelings and intuition when interpreting dream symbols. A dream guide may offer several interpretations of a symbol. Select the one that *feels* right.

A common dream experience is that of flying, or trying to fly. If you find yourself trying to fly in a dream but can't, it is likely that your subconscious is trying to tell you that there is some aspect of your life that "can't get off the ground." Another example is what I call the "vehicle dream." If you are driving a vehicle—car, train, bus, etc.—it is likely that you are in control of the aspect of life symbolized by the vehicle. If, however, someone else is driving and you are a passive passenger it may mean that you are not in control of that aspect of your life...someone else is. Observe who is in the driver seat of *your* dream vehicle!

If you suffer from nightmares, place one or more Rose Quartz gemstones in a soft pouch under your pillow. Children are particularly prone to nightmares at certain times of their development. Rose Quartz under their pillows will help prevent these nightmarish childhood dreamscapes.

Rose Quartz will help prevent bad dreams and bring on a peaceful night's sleep. Insert one or more pieces into a pouch and place under your pillow.

Children accept unquestioningly that Rose Quartz will prevent bad dreams. Adults are more skeptical and have to be convinced. When my niece and nephew were youngsters they would sometimes spend the night at my home. I used Rose Quartz to prevent their nightmares and calm their sleep. If I forgot to insert the gemstones under the pillow they would remind me. Rose Quartz proved so effective that I sent some home with them.

Chakra Balancing

Almost as relaxing as a massage and in some ways better, chakra balancing with gemstones is a wonderful therapy used to cleanse the aura, dissolve negative energy due to stress and tension, and return the chakras to proper functioning.

The word "chakra" is an Oriental term. The Western mystical counterpart of the chakras is referred to as an "energy center." Regardless of the words used to describe them, these centers are the psychic counterparts of physical glands and organs. They regulate and transmit energy entering your body from cosmic sources and the Earth's magnetic forces.

Due to stress, overwork, and other physical, mental, emotional, and psychic imbalances the energy centers may become unbalanced and unable to handle energy harmoniously. We become "out of sorts," tire easily, and are more susceptible to illnesses such as colds and flu.

The chakras—usually seven to twelve in number depending upon the tradition—rotate or spin in resonance with one another. If one is out of balance the others are affected. The chakras are generally agreed to be located in seven areas of the body. Following are their accepted locations and the colors associated with them:

1. At the base of the spine near the anus. Red.
2. In the region of the internal reproductive organs. Orange.
3. Near the solar plexus. Yellow.
4. In the vicinity of the heart. Green or sometimes pink.
5. Near the thyroid gland in the throat. Sky blue.
6. Between the eyebrows. Indigo blue.
7. At the crown of the head. Purple or violet—sometimes white.

OTHER USES FOR YOUR CRYSTALS AND GEMSTONES

Several minor energy centers are located in the hands and feet. The charkas have "openings" or portals at the front and back of the body on a horizontal line.

The energy and colors that some psychics and mystics see surrounding our bodies is referred to as the "aura." The aura is composed of the energies generated by the chakras, the frequencies of our emotions, beliefs, experiences, and fears, and the vibrations arising from body processes and thought forms.

Using crystals and gemstones from our divination set we can balance and redirect energy through the chakras.

Years ago I received a chakra balancing at an energy clinic and was spontaneously transported to what I can only describe as a past-life memory of living in a Tibetan monastery! It is not uncommon to experience an event such as this during a chakra balancing.

> The experience of chakra balancing is both relaxing and therapeutic to the one receiving the treatment and, to a lesser degree, the one giving it.

Long-repressed emotions and memories may also arise. While it is not possible to suffer physical injury or permanent psychological trauma during a chakra balancing, emotions and memories of trauma or abuse can arise. If this might be an issue, it is best to receive a chakra balancing from a trained energy therapist. It is possible to give yourself a chakra balancing too!

Gather the following stones from your divination collection: One each of Amethyst, Sodalite, Turquoise or Turqurenite, Malachite or Rose Quartz (or both Malachite and Rose Quartz), Citrine, Carnelian, Red Jasper, and two each of Quartz Crystal and Moss Agate.

For best results dim the lights. You may want to put on relaxing music and burn incense to help create the proper psychic conditions. Wear light, cotton clothing or only your underwear. Lie comfortably on the floor, a mat, or bed. Lying on grass will give you the benefit of both gemstone energies and Earth's magnetic energy.

It is easier to have someone apply the stones. However, as stated previously, you may also do this for yourself with a bit more effort. Lay the gemstones with their flattest side upon your skin. A small amount of petroleum jelly or olive oil can help a stone adhere better to bare skin on an area such as the forehead, chest, or belly.

Justin receives a chakra balancing using gemstones from a divination collection.

The stones are positioned thus:

1. Place an Amethyst Crystal so that it rests on the floor or pillow just touching the crown of your head. An Amethyst Tumble or Cabochon would be laid at the hairline.
2. Place the Sodalite on the Third Eye area between your brows.
3. Turquoise goes in the hollow of the throat.
4. Malachite and/or Rose Quartz rest upon the chest near or over the heart.
5. Citrine should be placed near the bellybutton.
6. Carnelian goes about four inches below the bellybutton in the region of the interior reproductive organs.
7. Red Jasper should lie upon the pubic bone.
8. Place each Moss Agate so that it rests against the bottom of each heel of your foot.
9. Each Quartz Crystal should lie in the palm of each hand.

OTHER USES FOR YOUR CRYSTALS AND GEMSTONES 171

After the stones have been positioned, lay quietly listening to music and allow yourself to drift into a relaxed, meditative state. You may feel some or all of your energy centers responding to the presence of the stones. Tingling, warmth or cooling and mild buzzing sensations are common.

Usually fifteen to forty-five minutes under the stones is sufficient. It is up to you whether you allow whoever applies the stones to stay quietly in the room or leave and gently close the door.

If you fear that uncomfortable emotions or memories may surface, you can choose to have someone present. The crystals and gemstones used not only balance and energize the charkas, they may also bring to the surface of your consciousness what needs to be addressed, faced, and dealt with.

My experience with chakra balancing has been that when painful emotions sometimes surface they are followed by peace and release. A peaceful, serene sleep often follows a chakra layout.

If you find that chakra balancing is something you would care to enjoy on a regular basis, you may want to read books (see *Sources* for titles) that specifically address the various methods and crystals used. You may also want to invest in larger crystals and gemstones mentioned in these books for deeper results.

However, you can give yourself or others a reasonably good chakra balancing using only the crystals and gemstones from your divination collection!

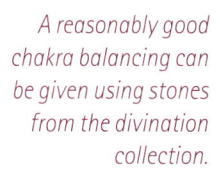

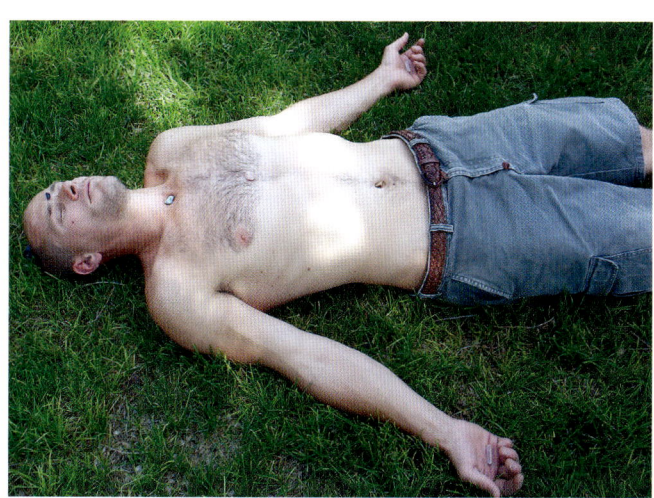

A reasonably good chakra balancing can be given using stones from the divination collection.

Amulets and Talismans

As mentioned previously, crystals and gemstones from your divination set may be worn to attract specific conditions into your life. Additionally, they can be worn for healing and protection.

A small, soft pouch—usually with a drawstring closure—such as in Native American or Celtic traditions—may be used to hold your stones for wearing. The pouch may be of fabric or hide. It may be knitted or crocheted. Patterns for knitted or crocheted amulet pouches or charm bags may be found at fabric stores (see the *Sources*). Look for amulet bags at New Age and magic shops.

An amulet bag makes wearing crystals and gemstones from your divination set easy and keeps them safe and secure from loss.

Let's say that you have been called upon to give a speech to a group of people. You want to control the butterflies in your stomach *and* you want to formulate your thoughts clearly and concisely to those to whom you will be speaking. In this case select one or more Turquoise or Aquamarine from your divination set. Place them in an amulet bag around your neck. You will want your amulet bag to rest as near the throat chakra as possible. Your bag may be worn under clothing, if you wish.

Agate and Jasper have long been worn for their grounding and courage-inducing properties. Wear Rose Quartz and Rhodocrosite near your heart when dealing with issues of love and forgiveness. These two gemstones will aid in healing a broken heart! Malachite acts to protect the heart from negative energies and emotions of the people in your sphere of activity. When traveling wear Quartz Crystal, Agates, or Jasper. Wear Aquamarine or Sodalite when taking a test or exam. Fossilized Dinosaur Bone and Citrine are a wonderful combination to wear when looking for your "right work" or seeking new employment. Clear Quartz Crystals may be worn or carried for all-purpose results when you are in a hurry and don't have time to consult a guide on specific gemstones.

> Any gemstone is energized and enhanced when paired with Quartz Crystal. Quartz Crystals also energize and protect your aura. People from many cultures including both my Cherokee and Celtic ancestors wore Quartz Crystals for their protective, energizing, and psyche-opening qualities.

Raising and Elevating Energy

One of the simplest ways to utilize the collective energy of your divination set is to merely set them out in a room. In whatever room you store your crystals and gemstones they will impart positive, rejuvenating energy to that space. When placed near plants your gemstone collection will energize and promote growth. You will also be raising the *individual* evolution potential for your plants.

My Cherokee ancestors used to purify water in cisterns, keeping it fresh and vital, by dropping in Quartz Crystals. There are more suggestions and techniques for using crystals and gemstones in water to make gemstone elixirs in Chapter 10—*Water Magnetism, Dowsing, and Gemstone Elixirs*.

If you have an indoor fountain you may wish to drop in several crystals or gemstones from your divination set. The water will be vivified and you will enhance the feng shui results that come by having a fountain in your environment. If you choose to use some of your divination crystals in an indoor fountain be sure you use distilled water in the fountain or your stones will be subject to mineral deposits.

By making the crystals and gemstones in your divination set a part of your daily life you will bring their healing, energizing effects into every facet of your affairs.

CHAPTER 9

Substitution and Gemstone Programming

WHETHER YOU CHOOSE TO COLLECT and polish crystals and gemstones from Nature or purchase them, you are likely to need to substitute for stones you can't find. The substitution information in Chapter 2—*The Hidden Messages of Crystals and Gemstones* will help you. You may also program gemstones to accept the message of those that prove unavailable.

When I began writing this book I quickly realized that some of the gemstones in my thirty-year old set, many of which I collected and polished myself, were either unavailable or have risen in cost to such a degree that acquiring them now is prohibitive. Therefore, in creating divination sets for others my need to substitute for costly or unavailable stones arose and continues to this day. Gemstone availability rises and falls as mining, fashion, politics, and rarity or abundance dictates.

When I put together my divination set decades ago, I used Fire Agate to represent the concept of "transformation" as this was its primary mineral message.

This lovely Fire Agate from my old divination set is now worth hundreds of dollars. Amegreen, which is also beautiful and carries a similar mineral message, is used in today's divination collections.

Fire Agate has become very pricey—sometimes costing hundreds of dollars for a small piece. Fire Agate is now too expensive for inclusion in the divination collection. It is no longer considered a "semi-precious" gemstone but now rivals precious gems in cost. Therefore Amegreen or Ametrine, which carry similar messages of "transformation," have been substituted for Fire Agate.

Turquoise too, has gone up in price. Turqurenite (dyed Magnesite) is an acceptable substitute.

Most "silica" gemstones may substitute—after programming—for those that prove unavailable during your search. Substitution stones may be imprinted or programmed by you with the needed message.

If you cannot find a particular gemstone suggested in this book, simply look for one of its substitutes—Chapter 2—*The Hidden Messages of Crystals and Gemstones*. However, this chapter cannot cover *all* the possibilities for gemstone substitution.

The Silica Factor

The mineral, silica, makes up ninety percent of the Earth's crust. Therefore, most crystals and gemstones contain this mineral. The properties of silica are amazing. It is what gives most crystals and gemstones the ability to store and transmit knowledge, energy, and information. It also allows them to be imprinted and programmed with additional information. Silica is the main component of Quartz Crystals, Agates, Jaspers, Chalcedonies, and Carnelian. Obsidian and Apache Tears are made of silica glass.

Most of the gemstones in the divination collection, with a few exceptions, are "silicates." This means that you may program or imprint them with thought and intention! You can also program them to retain any new messages and meanings you wish to add to your readings!

When substituting for stones you cannot find, in addition to the substitutions listed in Chapter 2, *Agates* are a safe bet. They contain silica and come in a wide variety of colors and patterns. Choose three that you feel will make a good substitute. Take them home, cleanse them, and imprint the desired message! You can also add stones to your divination collection that have messages you feel are relevant.

As an example, let's say you decide that you want to add three gemstones to your collection that have a meaning or message that is not presently included in this book. You decide that you want your three new stones to carry a message of the need to cultivate patience and mindfulness. You could refer to books on the subjects of healing and metaphysical aspects of gemstones and crystals to research gemstones that carry these or similar qualities. (Amber—fossilized tree resin—does carry a message of mindfulness and patience, by the way.) Or, you could explore New Age and mineral shops until you discover either crystals or gemstones that you *intuited* carried the particular message you want to add to your readings. However, this type of search can prove time consuming.

Far simpler would be to purchase three new Agates (all three of the same type, of course) that appeal to you and differ in color or pattern from those already in your collection. Through meditation and visualization simply imprint the new Agates with your desired message of patience and mindfulness.

During meditation, the new stones may reveal their inherent primary mineral message. You can choose to incorporate that message or imprint them to forgo that message in favor of the one that you wish instead. Another option, though slightly less expedient, is to program—as an example—Rose Quartz, already in your collection, to carry the new message of patience and mindfulness in addition to its inherent message of healing. Furthermore, you can program Rose Quartz, or any stones with multiple messages, to reveal to your consciousness which of several of their messages has relevance at the time of the reading.

> Generally, whichever message springs into your awareness first, or most clearly, is the one applicable at a given time.

Another manner in which a particular message reveals itself is that you may simply be unable to recall in a given moment unneeded messages. Yet, the most applicable one springs fresh and prominent into your mind. It seems that crystals and gemstones can induce temporary forgetfulness when required! The simplest method is simply to purchase and program three new stones with the message you wish to add to your collection.

Most, but not all of the stones in your divination set contain silica and may be programmed or imprinted. The exceptions to the programming/imprinting rule are Fluorite, Hematite, Magnesite, Malachite, Pyrite, Rhodocrosite (Rhodonite, while similar in composition to Rhodocrosite, *does* contain silica), and Turquoise (and Turqurenite).

178 CRYSTAL AND GEMSTONE DIVINATION

First vertical row are Rhodocrosite, Pyrite, and Turquoise. Middle row are Fluorite Octahedrons and Hematite. The third row consists of Magnesite, Turqurenite (Turquoise substitute) and Malachite. These gemstones, Fluorite, Hematite, Magnesite, Malachite, Pyrite, Rhodocrosite, and Turquoise (Turqurenite) cannot be programmed. Accept them as they are and value them for their unalterable mineral missions.

Accept these seven gemstones as they are. Value them for their particular properties and messages. These and other non-silicate stones play an important role in the evolution of the Earth and life on our planet. They hold in perpetuity, for as long as the Earth shall last, particular qualities and properties that must remain static in order to prevent evolution from going off on a radical tangent. These seven stones from the divination set (and other non-silicates) maintain order, symmetry, and pattern. They provide the stable foundation that supports and underpins the mutable and creative expressions of which evolution is capable, while keeping things from devolving into chaos and evolutionary anarchy.

While the mineral purpose of silica is to maintain lines of communication between all the diverse parts and purposes of the mineral realm and carry out ongoing programming in accordance with the pattern of evolution, the seven non-silicates in your divination set have other missions.

Said as simply as possible, and in accordance with my limited understanding of the greater, complex parts these seven play, the following applies:

Fluorite insures that the highest standards for evolution are maintained in accordance with the pattern issuing in a constant flow from Divine Mind.

Hematite brings stability and forms the foundation for life on our planet. It maintains the fundamental groundwork of the Divine pattern, subduing forces that would interfere with the basic foundation of life within and on the planet.

Magnesite maintains the karmic course of planetary evolution. This gemstone insulates and shields particular evolutionary processes from too rapid an acceleration. Think "process," "harmony," and "patience" in understanding the role of this gemstone's purpose.

Malachite aids in timely transformation in the processes of evolution and modulates the flow of electromagnetic energy within the body of the Earth.

Pyrite lays the foundation for succeeding evolutionary steps. Metaphorically, Pyrite guards the alchemical laws whereby lead is transformed into gold. This means that it prevents negative conditions from opposing the pure intent that lies behind the pattern of evolution of life on Earth set by Divine Mind.

Rhodocrosite maintains the vibration of unconditional love whereby the Divine creates within our realm of matter. It holds the ideal of Universal Love inviolate within the pattern of creation as a mirror holds an image resting before it.

Turquoise maintains a connection between the material and ephemeral aspects of creation. It maintains peace and equilibrium between density and spirit. You could say it reigns between heaven and earth and unites them. Turquoise holds and maintains the concept and vibration of peace.

While these seven gemstones do not become imprinted with negative programming or energy in the same manner as silicates, they still need cleansing of surface grime, oil, and dust. So do refresh them with a saltwater cleanse right along with the rest of the stones comprising your divination set.

Programming Crystals and Gemstones

If you think of a computer you will have an idea of what programming or imprinting a crystal or gemstone is all about. Of course, crystals and gemstones will not hold the amount or complexity of programming that computers will; still your stones will successfully retain the energy of any images, intentions, or purposes that you wish to imbue into them.

Give new silica gemstones that you intend to imprint a saltwater cleanse prior to programming as related in Chapter 7—*Acquiring and Caring for Your Crystals and Gemstones*. A saltwater soak only removes negative energy from handling and healing uses. It will not remove a stone's primary or programmed messages.

Mediation and visualization are the cornerstones of the imprinting process, and as suggested previously, set the stage for meditation. Now relax and hold in hand the three new Agates you wish to imprint. These could also be stones from your divination set that you want to reflect additional messages.

Close your eyes and concentrate upon the stones you are holding. See them in your mind's eye. If you wish to supplant an existing message with a new one ask silently that the former message be hidden—not deleted—but hidden or obscured from your consciousness during readings. After concentrating in this manner for a few moments begin to visualize the new message you wish to imprint. A few minutes may pass until you begin to feel the stones warming and gently vibrating.

This is your signal that the new imprinting has been accepted. Your newly programmed stones are now ready to add to your divination collection. It is helpful to record the new message in your notebook in addition to committing it to memory.

Depending upon how your readings unfold over time you may feel the need to add new categories of messages. Times change and so do the categories of mineral wisdom we need. If in your readings you find that a relevant category is missing, it may be time to acquire new stones and imprint them with relevant messages.

SUBSTITUTION AND GEMSTONE PROGRAMMING   181

Libbie programs an Amethyst Crystal. Her dog, Seamus, seems to be enjoying the meditation mood as well.

Adding Potential Message Categories

As mentioned earlier, patience or mindfulness is a category that is likely to become more relevant as our lives become increasingly busy and diversified. Other categories of mineral wisdom you may wish to add might be as follows:

1. Generosity.
2. Gratitude.
3. The need to decide between one or more options.
4. Victory or goals attained.

If you are a therapist you may wish to program and add stones that reflect more specifically your area of expertise. A psychologist may consider adding stones with programmed messages such as:

1. Childhood trauma
2. Spousal or parental abuse
3. Childhood fears
4. Dependency or co-dependency issues
5. Repressed memories

Spiritual counselors may want to consider adding crystals or stones that reflect the unique topics that their field covers.

People that have become non-responsive to others will often respond to the beauty and inherent vibrations of crystals and gemstones in much the same way as they would to friendly animals. Animals used for therapy do initiate responses in autistic children and in adults who have, for one reason or another, withdrawn from interaction. Crystals and gemstones will draw forth responses and interest. A patient may be attracted to particular gemstones. Watching which stones attract interaction will give a therapist vital clues to particular issues that a patient may be unable to verbalize or even remember. Look for visual clues revealed by which stones draw interest and interaction.

> The use of gemstones and crystals as part of a therapeutic model is a field that has great potential. When using a divination set in a therapeutic setting, the approach is not one of divination. In this case, the stones are used to suggest potentials to the therapist.

In a therapeutic setting the therapist takes notes of stones that are selected, held, touched, or moved about. Divination, per se, does not take place. The therapist merely observes and records the *potentials* revealed by the stones looking for clues.

The Power of Attraction

It is not uncommon to be wandering through a New Age shop or mineral marketplace and find yourself powerfully attracted by a particular type of stone or crystal. It may be that a stone or crystal has a personal message for you. It may also mean that the mineral realm itself wants to add a message to be conveyed in your readings to your divination set!

Being attracted *by* crystals or gemstones is one way that you may be called upon to add new facets of mineral wisdom to readings. This attraction can be very powerful. You may feel something pulling at you from across the room. Following the pull you find yourself standing over a tray of attractive gemstones. Next thing you know your hand has reached in and closed involuntarily around one or more of the stones.

Crystals and gemstones draw us through color, luster, beauty, and energy. Who could resist reaching for a lovely gemstone?

If you are paying attention you may feel a strong pulsation or sensation of warmth in your palm. You will not be happy or satisfied if you walk out of the shop without those particular stones! Heed the call and purchase them. If you don't, you will find yourself returning to the shop later that day or the next.

Meanwhile, while holding the gemstone or crystal that has attracted you try to get a feel for it and its energy. If possible, go within and ask why it drew you. Try to intuit its metaphysical or primary mineral message. Be assured that you *will* be able to intuit a stone's message, use, or meaning. Its *reason* for attracting you will be made known to you either at the shop or later during a gemstone meditation. If you are unsure of the message or your ability to intuit it, identify the name of the gemstone or crystal. Look for a label or ask the shop's proprietor the name of the stone. In a New Age store the proprietor will also be able to tell you something of the metaphysical properties, or you can look these up in books in the shop.

Sometimes simply looking up the definition of a stone can put you in harmony with its mineral message. Often a gemstone's message is very near its accepted New Age usage. Simply looking it up can put you in the right vibe to intuit its message and why it attracted your attention.

> If you discover that a new stone's message may be relevant to your readings you will want to purchase a set of three. After cleansing they will become a valued addition to your divination collection.

If you are unable to determine what the message or purpose of a gemstone is while in the store, purchase three anyway and take them home for more in-depth meditation or attunement work. It may be that conflicting energy from handling by customers or the comings and goings within the shop is interfering with your ability to attune to a stone's message.

With time, practice, communication—and trusting in your ability to communicate with other realms—you will be able to attune to any gemstone, anywhere, under any conditions. Soon you will discover that the mineral realm spontaneously communicates when you merely pick up and hold gemstones that attract, or that you are curious about.

Listening to Crystals and Gemstones

If you were unable to attune to the mineral message of your new gemstones, set the stage for meditation with the intention of *listening*. The act of listening to crystals and gemstones is different than programming or imprinting them. When programming or imprinting *you* select or program stones to fit your purposes. When you find yourself selected *by* gemstones and crystals its time to listen!

To *hear* the messages of stones that have *selected* you, set a meditation mood. Relax and hold your newly acquired, and cleansed, gemstones in your hand. Close your eyes and empty your mind of expectation, desire, or any attempt to "guess" what the stones wish to convey. Dismiss thoughts that arise. Shelve worries and concerns. Sit or lie quietly with your new stones resting in the palm of your hand.

Hold only the thought and image of the new stones in mind. Feel their weight in your hand. Ask them what they wish to convey to you. Then, release even this thought

Gemstones come in many pleasing shapes. Some will attract more than others. In the top row, left to right, are tumble polished fluorite pieces, a shaped fluorite "crystal" and fluorite octahedrons. In the second row are a variety of gemstone shapes available on the market, an oval cabochon, a small wand, a natural crystal, tumble polished stone and a natural "nugget." In the third row are natural pyrites or "rough" pieces and tumble polished pieces. Gemstones in any of these shapes and sheens make nice additions to your divination collection.

and wait in silence for the answer to come. As you open to the possibility of inter-realm communication, you will simultaneously find that your abilities to send *and* receive messages will sharpen.

In this book I have related the primary mineral messages of crystals and gemstones as they are used for divination. These primary messages are not the only wisdom crystals and gemstones have to impart! As you form bonds of communication and interaction with your stones you will become open to other messages and information they wish to impart.

In the next chapter I will give you techniques on how to magnetize water with thought and intention, how to "dowse" for auras, and use both water and the stones from your divination set to make healing and energizing elixirs!

CHAPTER 10

• • • • • • • • • •

Water Magnetism, Dowsing, and Gemstone Elixirs

IN THIS CHAPTER I WANT TO SHARE another wonderful technique for utilizing the crystals and gemstones from your divination set. In previous chapters you discovered the primary and Life Messages that the mineral realm has to share with humankind. You learned that during the health portion of any reading stones divulge information that may be of aid in helping prevent illness before it manifests in the physical body. Furthermore, the health reading offers up useful strategies that work in conjunction with professional (allopathic) and alternative health care regimens.

In addition to these wonder-filled uses stones from your divination set may be used for chakra balancing, meditation, visualization and manifestation of desires, and dreamwork! There are yet other extraordinary and helpful techniques whereby your divination stones will be of assistance to you.

Healing and Crystals and Gemstones

While I believe in the efficacy of crystals and gemstones to heal the physical body, I have reservations that merely *wearing* them is their best application when it comes to healing physical ailments.

Wearing stones does have a very positive effect upon the *energy* system of the body —particularly the aura. Therefore, the best technique to affect a physical healing is to route gemstone-energy through the human energy system of chakras and aura.

An important point to remember is—*in order for the mineral realm to heal a physical malady it must take an energetic route.* Wearing a stone, however, is not always the best way for its energy to be utilized by the body for healing.

> Can crystals and gemstones help us to heal? Yes! Yet, there are particular conditions that may need to be created if we are to use, to best advantage, their healing energies.

Simply wearing a crystal or gemstone will not always bring improvement to a physical malady. If you have an ailment you wish to affect using gemstone energy, try wearing a stone attuned to curing your malady. Wearing a stone for a month will give you an idea if there are going to be any results. If you don't receive improvement you may want to try making a crystal or gemstone elixir.

Treating a physical disease or illness *through* the energy portals, or chakras, or by ingesting the *energy*—but not the substance—of stones are viable therapies that aid physical healing. In this chapter I will illustrate how this may be accomplished with your divination stones or others that you purchase for healing purposes. First, let's look at why simply wearing a stone may not always work to heal a physical ailment.

Crystals, Gemstones and Physical Healing

First and foremost crystals and gemstones are inorganic. Yes, they have life, but they are inorganic life forms. Inorganic substances are not vibrationally attuned to heal an organic substance such as the human or animal body. Because the purpose of the mineral realm, first and foremost, is evolution, physical healing would be subsidiary to their primary function but can potentially arise out of it.

In the normal course of things there are very few minerals that organic life may consume without some process of alteration so that the body can assimilate and eliminate them. There are some single-cell life forms that utilize inorganic substances, but the more complex and diversified a body becomes, the less the inorganic-organic barrier can be breached.

Salt (Halite), a water-soluble mineral, is one of the minerals that can be assimilated. The human body can process salt and in fact needs it, but this assimilation process must have water to both absorb *and* eliminate it.

Aside from salt, most minerals when consumed in their natural state are insoluble, indigestible, and can be toxic. The vibrational field between organic and inorganic life is simply too vast to cross without some sort of mediator.

> For healing to occur we may need to employ mediators that can bridge the gap between the inorganic and organic realms making assimilation and healing more likely. These mediators are plants and water.

Plants remove insoluble minerals from the soil and convert them into forms that are easily absorbed for use within the human body. We eat plants and use them as medicine. Herbs are natural and holistic organic substances we may use to heal physical ailments. Pharmaceuticals are often made from, or isolated out of, organic substances into useful drugs. Drugs may also be made of inorganic substances that have been altered in such a manner as to be absorbable by the body—although sometimes they come with severe health risks and side affects. Even science has not completely or successfully bridged the gap between inorganic substances and the organic body.

> Water is an important vehicle for introducing the healing energies of crystals and gemstones into the body in a form that can be utilized.

Water—unless it has been distilled—naturally carries trace amounts of minerals that in most cases benefit the human body. Furthermore, water has "memory" and can absorb all types of energy signatures. We have an elemental affinity for water because we are in large part composed of water.

The homeopathic branch of medicine employs the capacity of water to "remember" and retain the energy signature of substances—plants and minerals—to which it has been exposed. As an example, the mineral Antimony is toxic to humans. However, when "potentized" by the homeopathic process the result is "Antimonium." This homeopathic remedy, which only retains the *energy* of Antimony and not its substance, makes a wonderful and harmless digestive aid for acid stomach. Water can aid us similarly in our quest to use crystals and gemstones for healing.

Water Magnetism and Gemstone Healing

Mystics and alchemists throughout the ages have understood the power of water to hold the imprint of substances to which it has been exposed. Merely exposing water physically to a substance or psychically to an idea is a simple technique for capturing energy signatures for healing and other purposes. This "potentized" water may be ingested or applied topically.

For interesting and illuminating information on the power of water to retain an idea or concept, read any of the books by the Japanese researcher, Masaru Emoto. I have listed two titles in the *Bibliography* at the back of this book. Mr. Emoto's research consists of taking water from a variety of sources—polluted and pristine sites alike. The water is then frozen and a thin layer removed and placed under a microscope to reveal the structure of ice crystals. These crystals are quickly photographed before they can melt. What is revealed is that water from polluted sites shows misshapen, incomplete crystals. Whereas frozen water from pristine natural sites reveals crystals that are sharp, beautiful and complete.

Furthermore, Mr. Emoto has shown that polluted water may be "healed" through the power of directed thought! Experiments in Japan indicate that polluted bodies of water can be healed by groups of people projecting both the *idea* and *intention* of healing. This is exciting stuff! An individual may also heal a vial of "damaged" water through thought projection.

Projecting thoughts of joy, love, kindness, gratitude, etc. may heal a vial of water that has shown poor crystal formation. After receiving these thought-forms the water is then frozen. The healed crystal structure reflects the beauty of the concepts engendered by these lofty thought vibrations. Healing water's capacity to create lovely ice crystals does not mean that one may purify polluted water sufficiently enough by thought alone to be able to drink it. It merely means that the energy structure of the water has been balanced. Interestingly, water subjected to

> What effects do our daily thoughts have upon the water composing our bodies? Are our daily thoughts geared toward healing? Or, are they causing damage within our bodies due to negative or hostile thought forms?

negative thought forms exhibits poor or malformed crystal structures. Something to think about is that the human body is about seventy percent water.

The ancient knowledge of the memory of water has been retained by mystics, alchemists and others and is again being made available for the benefit of all people worldwide. The ancients called the process of programming the memory of water, "water magnetism."

Alchemists also called water "the Universal Solvent" not only because it could literally dissolve and wear away something as enduring as stone but because it was used in many of their laboratory procedures. They understood that merely by contact with a substance, water could absorb the energy signature of that substance *without* any diminishment to the source-substance.

It is the concept of water memory and magnetism that will provide one of the methods whereby we can use crystals and gemstones for healing. We will be utilizing crystals and gemstones and water-magnetism to create healing and energizing elixirs from the crystals and stones in your divination collection.

Water Magnetism and Gemstone Elixirs

It is possible to magnetize water with thought alone. Fill an eight ounce glass (be sure it is made of glass) and cradle it between your palms. The palm of one hand should be over the top of the glass and the other palm supporting the glass from the bottom. For three or four minutes breathe deeply and slowly, filling the lungs and then completely expelling the air before taking the next breath.

Holding your glass of water, project a thought such as "healing" or "energy" or whatever you want to imbue. After focusing for about three minutes upon the water, drink the entire contents of the glass. If you do this before bed you may feel a slight tingling throughout your body. You will have received the tonic effect of the magnetized water that will gradually dissipate over the next several hours.

> Comfortable, deep, rhythmic inhalations and exhalations will allow you to concentrate upon the message you want to program into the water. Your eyes may be open or closed during the magnetizing process.

If you want more lasting effects making a gemstone elixir is simple and effective. Gemstone elixirs are made similarly to homeopathic flower remedies. Select the gemstone that embodies the healing energy you desire (see the *Bibliography* for books containing gemstone healing qualities). I have also listed a brief synopsis of the healing properties of the stones from your divination set for your convenience. This list is by no means a complete inventory of all the curative properties of your divination stones but is sufficient to get you started.

Be sure the crystal or gemstone you select has been cleansed and set in the sun to energize and dry. You will want to sit in meditation with the stone and *ask* that it participate in your healing. The act of asking is a simple technique of opening inter-realm communication. Asking creates *intention*. Intention stimulates energy toward your desire.

Furthermore, define the type of healing you desire. Most stones have vibrations that affect more than one aspect of a person's energy system. Be specific in visualizing what area of your body requires healing.

Place the chosen stone from your divination collection into a clean glass container such as a Mason jar (eight to sixteen ounces in volume) and fill with distilled water. You need only one stone, and size is not an issue when making elixirs. Your divination stones are a good size for elixir making. This is a case where bigger is not better. It is the *energy* of a stone that is important,

By making a crystal or gemstone elixir, essential healing energies are made available for more potent healing results.

not size. Secure a piece of cheesecloth (to keep the dust and bugs out) over the opening of your jar with a rubber band. Place this outside in a sunny spot for two to four hours preferably during the hours of 8:00 a.m. and 12:00 noon. The morning hours are best because positive Earth-energies are at their peak.

While you are in physical contact with the stone and water-filled jar try to hold in mind the healing you are seeking.

After the elixir has completed its exposure to the morning sun, decant the water and remove the stone returning it to your divination set. The stone's energy is in no way depleted and may be used for other purposes and, of course, divination. Your elixir may be stored in a cupboard or pantry. Shake the jar to animate the gemstone energy and pour out about two ounces for consumption. Take the elixir several times a day in two-ounce doses after shaking to "excite" the energy.

> Don't think about the negative aspects of your ailment or concentrate upon your symptoms. Instead, visualize healing and a return to health. See yourself healed of your malady.

If you want to further potentize your elixir, first make one using a clear Quartz Crystal from your divination set. With the resulting crystal water make an elixir in the usual manner using a stone that resonates with the type of healing you seek. In the case of skin maladies elixirs may be applied topically in addition to ingesting them.

When making gem elixirs it is possible to add color-energy for varying effects. Purchase a collection of various colors of translucent plastic or glass sheets. Select the one that most meets your healing or energy needs and place it over the top or propped against the side of the jar while your elixir is soaking up the sun's rays. The colored sheet can replace the cheesecloth in order to keep out dust but may need to be secured with tape so it doesn't blow off. Another method is to set your jar upon a square of colored felt, fabric, or paper. Refer to Chapter 8—*Other Uses for Your Crystals and Gemstones* for information on color properties.

Gemstones and the mysterious capacity of water to absorb energy combine to create an effective method whereby mineral-energy may be introduced into the body for the purposes of healing.

Healing Properties of Gemstone Elixirs

Following is a brief list of the healing properties of the crystals and gemstones in your divination collection. As with other types of medicine, gemstone elixirs are not cure-alls. There is no plant, mineral, or potion that cures every ailment all of the time. Gemstone elixirs enhance and work well with other healing methods. **When using gemstone elixirs, always use them in conjunction with professional medical care, especially for serious or life threatening ailments.**

Elixirs will not diminish the effects of medicines, drugs, or herbs, nor will they create negative side effects when used in combination with other therapies. **Do not use gemstone elixirs as a substitute for seeking medical attention!**

A further caveat is to never make an elixir with a mineral that is grainy in texture, has loose material, or is soluble in water. Solid crystals and tumble polished nodules, beads, or cabochons—such as the stones recommended for your divination collection—are safe to use for making gemstone elixirs. They will impart their energy without imbuing your elixir with insoluble matter. Stones, such as Serpentine and Tiger Eye from your divination set that contain minerals such as asbestos are safe to use because that mineral is insoluble within a silica matrix.

Amethyst—Aids the development and projection of self-esteem, has a mild tonic effect upon the lungs, opens psychic sight to the devic and spiritual realms, and aids in living a holistically integrated life.

Amegreen—This stone combines the vibrations of both Amethyst and Green Quartz. See Amethyst and Citrine (the effects of Green Quartz are similar) for effects of this gemstone in elixir form.

Apache Tear—Aids digestion and has a tonic effect upon muscle tissue, cools inflammation issues, and helps dissolve deep-seated grief.

Aquamarine—An elixir of this gem also enhances self-esteem but in a more overt manner than Amethyst. It aids in the expression of courage and strength in the face of adversity. It tones the liver, kidneys, spleen, and thyroid.

Bloodstone—Detoxifies the system and aids in conditions of inflammation, blood disorders, and tones the heart chakra.

Blue Lace Agate—Balances brain fluid and aids hydrocephalic conditions. Helps dissolve long-held anger. Allows the throat chakra to process and handle higher frequencies of spiritual energy.

Carnelian—This gemstone has a tonic effect upon the blood allowing it to carry more energy. It aids in developing a positive and courageous outlook on life and in softening and passing gallstones. Makes one more "magnetic" personality-wise.

Citrine—Nourishment of female organs and adrenals results from an elixir made from this gemstone. It also aids PMS and menopausal symptoms, hot flashes, and balances hormones that cause these problems.

Crazy Lace Agate—This elixir strengthens capillaries to better transmit blood cells, aids in skin conditions, and tones blood circulation.

Dalmatian Agate—Aids in the assimilation of Vitamins E and B.

Fluorite—Strengthens tooth enamel and gum tissues and eases inflammation in the mouth. There is a tonic effect upon the lung tissue and heightened immunity to viral infections and pneumonia.

Fossilized Dinosaur Bone—Take this elixir in combination with homeopathic silica or infusions (herbal teas) of horsetail herb to aid in the building up of jaw and bone tissue and dental enamel during and after menopause. This gem elixir will aid in the assimilation of silica and calcium from food and herbs.

Girasol—Balances liquid ratios in the body, tones the lymphatic system. For best effect pair this elixir with gentle exercise such as yoga, walking, or Tai Chi.

Hematite—Increases blood cell production and aids in correcting blood disorders.

Labradorite—This elixir has a toning and cleansing effect upon the aura and dissipates stress, tension, and fear.

Lepidolite—Aids in the alleviation or balancing of menopausal symptoms and stimulates healing energy in regards to dental problems.

Lined Agate—Tones digestion.

Magnesite— Aids in finding joy in present circumstances.

Malachite—Aids mental disturbances such as autism, epilepsy, physical and mental imbalances. An elixir of this stone helps to relieve toxicity and conditions caused by radiation exposure.

Moonstone—Aids insomnia, sleepwalking, awakens psychic powers and spirituality, calms and reduces depression.

Moss Agate—Helps the absorption of nutrients, reduces nervous tension, and balances blood sugar levels. Also aids in appreciating one's present circumstances.

Pink Aventurine—Balances mind, body, and emotional interaction. This elixir also benefits the lungs, brain, and liver. It is calming and de-stressing. Use with herbal infusions of milk thistle, dandelion, sage, mugwort, or motherwort. This elixir treats the energy-body while the herbs treat the physical symptoms in a symbiotic manner.

Pyrite—Soothes "hot" emotions and helps eliminate the fear that often hides behind anger. This elixir assists in inflammatory conditions such as swelling and rashes.

Quartz Crystal—Energizes and expands the aura, energizes other gem elixirs, and has a positive, tonic effect on all body and energy systems.

Red Jasper—Stimulates reproductive organs and blood components. It eliminates negative vibrations and energies from the aura. Also adds the important orange light wave to the aura, increasing one's personal magnetism.

Rhodocrosite—Make this elixir with crystal water and expose it to the orange light wave using an orange plastic, glass, fabric, or paper sheet to make a potent but calming heart healer and energizer.

Rhodonite—This elixir benefits physical hearing and the inner ear. It also aids with psychic hearing and the absorption of Vitamins A, B, and E.

Rose Quartz—Stimulates the parasympathetic systems and ganglia, and the heart, kidneys, lungs, and liver. It increases fertility, especially in males. It also stimulates artistry and creativity.

Red Tiger Eye—Strengthens mental health and stabilizes functions related to the heart and root chakra.

Serpentine—Aids in awakening Kundalini energy at the base of the spine. It also balances the organs and glands that are the physical counterparts of the chakras. Helps one to attain psychic vision and is said to "magnetize" one's aura toward the finding of treasure!

Snowflake Obsidian—Helps to improve one's sexual and gender image. Balances the operation of the digestive system, tones muscle tissue, aligns mental and emotional bodies, and reduces stress and tension.

Sodalite—Strengthens the lymphatic system, especially when combined with exercise. This elixir reduces stress, aids emotional balance and spiritual growth. It also eases the symptoms and harm caused by radiation exposure.

Sunstone—Stimulates a sunny, joyful outlook on life.

Tiger Eye—Used with other gems as an energizer similarly to Quartz Crystal.

Turquoise—Energizes all systems, aids with nutrient absorption, heals and repairs connective tissue, and protects against environmental contaminants and cosmic radiation. This elixir aids oxygen absorption and helps protect against solar radiation when taken several weeks before ascending to high altitudes. Also aids in maintaining a joyful, peaceful outlook on life. Turqurenite when used in elixir making will have the same attributes as Magnesite.

Turritella Agate—Stimulates digestion and relieves acid reflux, especially when combined with eating less fat, more fiber, and decreasing portion size. Furthermore, it is strengthening to all physical functions and the skeletal system.

Unakite—Calming, de-stressing and an aid when working through rebirthing techniques. Also helps recovery from chronic illness.

Yellow Quartz—Regenerates and tones the endocrine tissue, especially the thymus and pancreas. This elixir is also an excellent detoxifier.

You don't need to wait for a physical ailment to incorporate gemstone elixirs into your health regimen! Besides medicinal uses, elixirs have psychic and spiritual effects. They aid in developing courage, self-esteem, personal magnetism, and other positive and useful characteristics. For a complete list of the healing energies of crystals and gemstones, refer to the *Bibliography* for some excellent book titles.

Dowsing and Auric Enhancement

The aura of a healthy individual extends several feet outward from the body.

The same is true of someone who meditates and incorporates a spiritual aspect into his or her life. An unhealthy aura may extend only a few inches or be nearly non-existent.

The aura is a premier reflection of our health. It mirrors the emotions and beliefs we indulge in.

Why will an assailant attack one person and not another? Often it is the unconscious perception of the condition of one's aura. Does an aura reflect vitality and self-assurance? Or, does it project weakness and vulnerability?

> Our auras protect us from negative energy and psychic assault. A healthy, vibrant aura may even protect against physical assault!

An attacker will *instinctively* choose a victim with a weak aura or diminished projection of energy. This is why one may successfully wear crystals and gemstones for protection. Protection is more about the projection of energy than it is of physical strength or size.

A healthy aura deflects negative energy and illness. It is important to maintain a strong, vibrant aura. Diet, exercise, meditation, moderation in all things (balance) and an optimistic and positive outlook aid in developing an expansive and protective aura. Ingesting gemstone elixirs will expand the strength and size of the aura. So will wearing crystals and gemstones. It is easier to prevent illness than to cure it once it manifests. Wearing crystals and gemstones expands the dimensions and potency of the aura thereby helping to prevent illness. Once illness is contracted, gemstone elixirs deliver the greatest levels of healing energy in a form easily assimilated.

Most people, except under ideal lighting conditions can see but a portion of the aura that lies closest to the body. This often appears as a grayish outline. Yet anyone can measure the strength of the aura with an "aurameter" or dowsing rods. An aurameter (see *Sources*) is an exceptionally sensitive type of dowsing rod that easily measures the outer boundary of one's aura. It is usually made of copper, chrome-nickel, or gold plated. The late Dowsing Master, Verne L. Cameron, developed and named the *Original Cameron Aurameter* during the 1950s.

An aurmeter measures subtle energy fields emanating from the body.

With an aurameter anyone can measure one's own aura or that of someone else without needing the ability to *see* the aura. To measure someone's aura stand about twenty feet in front of the one being measured. Hold the aurameter and slowly advance toward the person. The meter will swing strongly backward toward the operator when it encounters the edge of an aura (it also measures other types of energy fields, as well).

To measure your own aura simply stand facing a wall at a distance of about fifteen or twenty feet. Walk toward the wall. When the outer edge of your aura hits the wall the meter will swing backward strongly and decisively.

Any substance that causes an allergic reaction or has a weakening effect upon the body, such as cigarettes, alcohol, drugs, negative thoughts or emotions and synthetic foods and substances, will vastly diminish one's aura.

An aura is strengthened by positive thoughts, meditation, healthy foods, exercise, and *wearing a crystal or gemstone*! Wearing a crystal or gemstone instantly increases the diameter of one's aura, often doubling it in diameter. Wearing or carrying a crystal or gemstone not only increases the diameter of one's aura but also increases it in vitality and intensity.

This then is the most important reason to wear a crystal or gemstone—protection and an increase in one's personal energy field.

How does one select the best crystal or gemstone for enhancing one's personal energy field?

The best method is to use an aurameter, dowsing rods, or a pendulum. Your divination kit will handily provide you with thirty-eight different types of gemstones to test! Take a baseline reading of the diameter of yours or another's aura *without* wearing any

200 CRYSTAL AND GEMSTONE DIVINATION

The aurameter reveals that Justin has a normal, healthy aura.

Justin holds an Amethyst Crystal to see if this is his best option for energizing his aura.

gemstones. Then one at a time select and hold, or have your subject hold, a stone from your divination set and test the aura noting the diameter by which each of the stones causes an increase. The best stone for wearing is the one that gave the most beneficial boost to the aura.

And don't forget your pets! Pets, too, benefit from wearing crystals and gemstones.

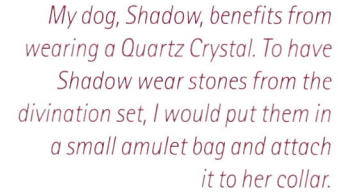

My dog, Shadow, benefits from wearing a Quartz Crystal. To have Shadow wear stones from the divination set, I would put them in a small amulet bag and attach it to her collar.

The ancients knew that gemstones and crystals have favorable effects upon one's personal energy field. The famous breastplate of Aaron was encrusted with twelve stones well known for their empowering and protective energies. Shamans, priests, warriors, hunters, medicine men and women, and children all wore crystals or gemstones to imbue their personal energy with that of particular mineral properties. One would be hard pressed to point out a culture that did not utilize the energies of crystals and gemstones for a variety of purposes including divination!

In the earliest days of human culture stones may have been worn or employed first and foremost for their energy properties. Secondly, they were used to make useful, functional tools. Adornment may have been only an afterthought. Or, perhaps the beauty and adornment potentials are how the mineral realm first drew humans into contact! Today we are rediscovering that in addition to personal ornamentation there are many wonderful reasons to wear, carry, or in other ways avail yourself of crystal and gemstone energies.

Throughout our journey into the mineral realm you have witnessed and learned amazing things! Not only are crystals and gemstones willing and able to communicate with you—and you with them—you have learned how to tune into their messages on life, health, love, prosperity, the future and more! You now understand how to easily channel their evolutionary energies for healing by making and using gem elixirs. Furthermore, you know how mineral-energies can help you manifest your personal goals and desires! You have learned that simply by wearing a crystal or gemstone from your divination set you can immediately enhance and strengthen your aura as an aid to protection and mitigation of illness.

It is my hope that you will persist on your journey of discovery, continuing and maintaining the connection you have forged with the mineral realm and the practical application of skills shared within these pages. Through these methods you have turned a key in the lock of a long-closed door of inter-realm communication. I hope you will continue to enhance your life via daily contact with the light of the stars as manifested within the mineral realm!

Karma Cat and gemstones.

Glossary

Amulet—A gem, written spell, or ornament worn as a charm to achieve a condition.

Aura—An invisible energy emanation surrounding the bodies of living things.

Aurameter—A sensitive dowsing rod for measuring subtle energy emanations.

Cabochon—A stone cut in a convex shape but not faceted.

Chakras—Energy centers within the human or animal body.

Divination—An act or method of foretelling future events and conditions.

Elixir—A "tincture" or medicine.

Findings—Metallic connecting pieces and settings for jewelry.

Igneous—Pertaining to or having the nature of fire.

Lapidary—One who cuts, engraves, and polishes stones and gems.

Metamorphic—Pertaining to physical transformation.

Querist—One receiving a divination.

Sedimentary—pertaining to the deposit of sediment.

Semi-precious stones—Stones that are less valuable than those called "precious."

Tumble polishing—Batch polishing of stones to achieve shine and smooth edges. Tumble polished stones are sometimes called, "baroques" because of their non-uniform shapes.

Visualization—The art and practice of seeing with the "mind's eye."

Water-soluble—That which dissolves in water.

BIBLIOGRAPHY

Gem Elixirs and Vibrational Healing, Vol. 1, by Gurudas, Cassandra Press, Boulder, Colorado: 1985

Minerals of the World, by Charles A. Sorrell, Golden Press, NY, New York: 1973

Simon & Schuster's Guide to Rocks & Minerals, by Prinz, Harlow, and Peters, Simon & Schuster, New York, New York: 1977

Rocks and Minerals, by Herbert Zim and Paul Shaffer, Golden Press, New York, New York: 1957

The Secret Life of Water, by Masaru Emoto, Atria Books, New York, New York: 2005

Ancient Gems, by J. Henry Middleton, Argonaut Inc., Publishers, Chicago, Illinois: 1969

Cunningham's Encyclopedia of Crystal, Gem & Metal Magic, by Scott Cunningham, Llewellyn Publications, St. Paul, Minnesota: 1991

The Hidden Messages in Water, by Masaru Emoto, Beyond Words Publishing, Inc., Hillsboro, Oregon: 2004

Love is in the Earth: A Kaleidoscope of Crystals, by Melody, Earth-Love Publishing House, Wheatridge, Colorado: 1991

The Crystal Bible, by Judy Hall, Walking Stick Press, Cincinnati, Ohio: 2003

Healing With Crystals and Gemstones, by Daya Sarai Chocron, Samuel Weiser, Inc., York Beach, Maine: 1986

Crystal Enlightenment: Transforming Properties of Crystals and Healing Stones, Vol. I, By Katrina Raphaell, Aurora Press, New York, New York: 1985

Crystal Healing: The Therapeutic Application of Crystals and Stones, Vol.II, by Katrina Raphaell, Aurora Press, New York, New York: 1987

You Can Heal Your Life, by Louise L. Hay, Hay House, Inc., Santa Monica, CA: 1984

The Dream Book: Symbols for Self-Understanding, by Betty Bethards, Inner Light Foundation, Novato, California: 1983

SOURCES

Auroshikha Incense
Imported by:
Auroma Int'l, Inc.
Silver Lake, WI 53170
USA
An aromatic incense made in Pondicherry, India at the Sri Aurobindo Ashram, using only herbs, flowers, and essential oils.

Bombay Incense Company
P.O. Box 915802
Longwood, FL 32791-5802
www.newageimports.com; toll-free 1-866-47-NEWAGE

American School of Needlework, Inc.
ASN Publishing
1455 Linda Vista Drive
San Marcos, CA 93069
USA
Crochet Little Amulet Bags
This pattern book has 12 designs for beaded and crocheted amulet bags.

Gem Guides Book Company
Baldwin Park, CA
USA
www.gemguidesbooks.com
Publisher and Distributor of books on crystals, minerals and gems, beads and jewelry crafts, and *Recreational Gold Prospecting for Fun and Profit*, by Gail Bulter.

eBay.com
Lapidary equipment, crystals and gemstones.

Gail's Garden of Gems
Offering dried mugwort herb for sale and "Ask the Author" for on-going advice and support.
www.gailsgardenofgems.com

The Original Cameron Aurameter
www.dowsing.com/Dowsing/orig...com.htm

INDEX

Alchemists, 191
Amegreen
   and divination, 19–21
   and Tarot, 127
Amethyst
   and divination, 18–19
   and manganese, 18
Amulet
   stones for, 172–173
Amulets, 172–173
Ancestors, 1, 2, 4, 8, 21, 38, 40, 58, 60, 173
Ancients, the
   and the mineral realm, 8
Apache Tear
   and divination, 21–22
   and Tarot, 128
Aquamarine
   and divination, 22–23
   and Tarot, 128
Architecture
   and cultural development, 8–9
   and mono-culture, 9
Attunement
   first step to, 2

Aura
   as a reflection of health, 198
   measuring, 198–199
   strengthening, 199–201
Aurameter, 198–201
Barter
   as payment, 76
Birthrights
   ancient, 2
Bloodstone
   and divination, 24
   and Tarot, 129
Blue Lace Agate
   and divination, 25
   and Tarot, 129
Books
   how-to, 144
Cameron, Verne L.
   and the aurameter, 198
Carnelian
   and divination, 25–26
   and Tarot, 129
Casting the stones, 63
Cats
   and crystals and gemstones, 3–4

INDEX

Chakra balancing, 150, 154–156, 168–171, 187–188
    using crystals and gemstones, 169
Chakras
    counterparts of physical glands and organs, 168
Channel
    to the mineral realm, 4
Citrine
    and divination, 26–27
    and Tarot, 130
Color
    and cosmic vibration, 163–164
Conscious awareness
    domination by, 80
Crazy Lace Agate
    and divination, 27–28
    and Tarot, 130
Crystal Index
    to illustrate gemstone layouts, 72–75
Crystals and gemstones
    acquiring, 143–147
    and Moonlight, 150–151
    and New Age shops, 145
    and pets, 145
    buying online, 147
    cleansing, 147–154
    effects upon energy centers, 7–8
    incorporating into life, 5
    influence on life, 5–6
    polishing and shaping, 7
    traveling with, 158
Dalmatian Agate
    and divination, 28–29
    and Tarot, 130
Dialog
    inter-realm, 2
Divination, 6–7, 15, 17–62, 63–76, 77, 80–95, 97, 125–126, 141, 143–158

Divination (continued) 159–162, 169, 172–173, 175–186, 187–202
Divination stones
    sizes of, 63–64
Dowsing rods, 198–201
Dream guides, 167
Dreams, 4, 45, 119, 165–168
    recording, 167
Dreamwork, 165–168
Drugs, 44, 190, 194
    and side effects, 190
Earth's alchemy, 149
Earth-processes, 5–6, 11–15
    action of wind and water, 11
    giving rise to crystals and gemstones, 11
Ebay, 144
Egyptians
    and architecture, 9
Elements
    and their functions, 9–11
    combinations of, 5
    within minerals, 9
Elixir
    potentizing, 193
Emoto, Masaru
    water research, 190
Energy
    from handling, 150
    imprinting, 149
Equipment
    lapidary and tumble polishing, 144
Ethics
    and gemstone readings, 72
Ficino, Marsilio, 15
Findings, 147
Fluorite
    and divination, 29–30
    and Tarot, 131

Fossilized Dinosaur Bone
    and divination, 30–31
    and Tarot, 131
Gem Guides Book Company, 143
Gemstone elixirs
    and the aura, 155
    healing properties, 194–197
Gemstone-energies
    blocking, 7
Gemstones
    artificially colored, 150
    effect on individual consciousness, 6–7
    using with intention, 6–7
    wearing for adornment, 6–7
Gemstones and crystals
    color enhancing, 150
    used in therapy, 182
Girasol
    and divination, 32
    and Tarot, 131–132
Greeks, the
    art and architecture, 8
Healing, 7, 8, 13, 17, 20, 22, 34, 36, 41, 49, 50–51, 56–57, 88, 104–105, 106, 117, 122–123, 138, 145, 147–148 157, 161–162, 163, 164, 172, 173, 187–191, 193, 194–197
    and gemstone elixirs, 191–197
Health reading, 20–21, 33, 39, 44, 50, 51, 67, 77, 105–109, 115–116, 119–120, 188
Hematite
    and divination, 33
    and Tarot, 132
Herb bundles
    for smudging, 154
Herbs
    crystal and gemstone cleansing, 147–154

Herbs (continued)
    for healing, 189
Igneous rocks, 13
Incense
    for cleansing gemstones, 153
    to use, 153
Labradorite
    and divination, 34
    and Tarot, 132
Law of the Triangle, 48, 160
Law, the, 160–163
Lepidolite
    and divination, 35
    and Tarot, 133
Lined Agate
    and divination, 35–36
    and Tarot, 133
Magnesite
    and divination, 37
    and Tarot, 133
Malachite
    and divination, 37–39
    and Tarot, 134
Manganese
    and quartz, 18
Manifestation, 48, 131, 160–162, 188
    of desires, 161–162
Marble
    and the Greeks, 8
Mediators
    plants and water, 190–191
Meditation, 6–7, 18, 63, 80, 145, 148, 155, 159–164, 177, 180, 184, 187
    creating a mood for, 161–162
Metamorphic rocks, 14
    and transformation, 14
Mineral consciousness, 1
    and inter-realm communication, 1

Mineral life
  inorganic and inanimate, 1
Mineral realm
  and humanity, 1
Mineral shows
  and crystals and gemstones, 145, 146
Mineral-human connection, 1
Minerals
  and communication, 1
  and the evolution of the Earth, 5-6
  daily use of, 6
  frequencies of, 6
  in crystals and gemstones, 6-7
  memory and mission, 6
  useful properties, 6
Minerals and ores
  alloys of, 6
Missions
  of gemstones, 179
Moonstone
  and divination, 39-40
  and Tarot, 134
Moss Agate
  and divination, 40-41
  and Tarot, 134
Mugwort
  acquiring, 150-151
  and saltwater soak, 150
  as a digestive aid, 150-151
Mystics, 168, 191
Nightmares,
  and Rose Quartz, 167-168
Nine-stone layout, 66
Pad
  edges of, 100
Physical senses
  and psychic counterparts, 17
Pink Aventurine
  and divination, 42

Pink Aventurine (continues)
  and Tarot, 135
Polarity, 10, 160
Polluted water
  healing of, 190
Programming
  crystals and gemstones, 180
  the memory of water, 190
Prosperity
  increasing, 160
Pyrite
  and divination, 43-44
  and Tarot, 178
Quantum field, 162
Quartz Crystal
  and divination, 44-45
  and Tarot, 135
  attraction to, 3-4
Quartz crystal cluster
  energizing gemstones with, 156
Quartz crystals
  and the Cherokee, 4
Questions
  negative answers to, 95
Rain
  exposing stones to, 155
Reading the pad, 99-102
  stone placement, 101-102
Reading.
  and money, 76
Red Jasper
  and divination, 46
  and Tarot, 136
Red Tiger Eye
  and divination, 47-48
  and Tarot, 136
Rhodochrosite
  and divination, 48-49
  and Tarot, 137

Rhodonite
    and divination, 49–50
    and Tarot, 137
Rock shops
    and crystals and gemstones, 145
Romans, the
    and architecture, 8–9
Rose Quartz
    and divination, 50–51
    and Tarot, 138
Sagan, Carl, 15
    and star stuff, 15
Salt
    a water soluble mineral, 188
    kosher, 148
    sea, 148
    table, 148
Saltwater
    soaking crystals in, 148–149
Sandstone
    and the Egyptians, 9
Science, 1–2, 5–6
Sedimentary rock, 12
Self-readings, 77–95
    and gemstone communication, 77
Serpentine
    and divination, 51–52
    and Tarot, 138
Seven Wonders of the World
    and the Great Pyramid, 9
Silica, 14, 176–179
Silicate family
    of minerals, 3
Silicates
    in the divination collection, 176–179
Skepticism
    suspending, 4
Snowflake Obsidian
    and divination, 52–53

Snowflake Obsidian (continued)
    and Tarot, 138
Sodalite
    and divination, 53–54
    and Tarot, 139
Spirit energy, 127, 160
Stone
    sun energizing, 149, 155
Stone Age, 8
Stones
    air drying, 149
    effect on energy system, 188
    group messages of, 81
    in closely related groups, 69
    relating names of, 99
    wearing as an amulet, 163
Sunstone
    and divination, 54–55
    and Tarot, 139
Tea
    mugwort, 150–151
Thoughts
    effect on water, 190–191
    projecting, 190
Tiger Eye
    and divination, 55–56
    and Tarot, 139
Turquoise
    and Divination, 56–57
    and Tarot, 140
Turritella Agate
    and divination, 57–58
    and Tarot, 140
Unakite
    and divination, 58–59
    and Tarot, 141
Universe
    leaving details to, 161

INDEX

Visualization
    and realization, 161
Volcanic ash
    and the Romans, 8
Water
    affinity for, 189
    and memory, 189
    as the Universal Solvent, 191

Water (continued)
    frozen, 190
    magnetizing, 190
Water magnetism, 190–193
Yellow Quartz
    and divination, 59–60
    and Tarot, 141

About the Author

Of Celtic and Cherokee heritage, Gail Butler has had a fascination with all aspects of the natural and mystical worlds. The mysteries of the mineral realm, in particular, have been a lifelong study

Gail is a well-known and respected gold prospector and mineral hunter, as well as an experienced lapidary artist. She has taught rockhounding and gold prospecting classes, lectured on the art of gold prospecting to clubs and organizations, written numerous articles for various publications and was a contributing editor for *Rock & Gem Magazine* for over twenty years.

Her metaphysical background includes membership in the Rosicrucian Order, AMORC, for over twenty years and summer studies in alchemy and other subjects at the Rose Croix University in San Jose, California. She is also a member of the Fellowship of Isis, Crossroads Lyceum, and past member of the Philosophers of Nature, a group devoted to the study of alchemy and the laws of Nature.

Gail has had two previous books published, *Rockhounding California* (Globe Pequot) and *Recreational Gold Prospecting for Fun and Profit* (Gem Guides Book Company). This present book combines her extensive knowledge of both the physical and metaphysical properties and aspects of the mineral kingdom.

Gail retired from the Los Angeles County Sheriff's Department in 1993 where she worked as a Deputy Sheriff for twenty years. She was born in San Gabriel, California, and now resides in Utah.

Gail offers on-going advice and support at www.gailsgardenofgems.com "Ask the Author."